THE A-Z OF

CW00460039

COUNTY CORK

STRANGE
STORIES OF
MYSTERIES,
CRIMES AND
ECCENTRICS

KIERAN McCARTHY

The
History
Press

Dedicated to my niece, Katie, may you forever smile.

First published 2023

The History Press
97 St George's Place, Cheltenham,
Gloucestershire, GL50 3QB
www.thehistorypress.co.uk

British Library Cataloguing in Publication Data.
A catalogue record for this book is available from the British Library.

978 1 80399 048 4

Typesetting and origination by The History Press.
Printed and bound in Great Britain by TJ Books Limited, Padstow, Cornwall.

Trees for LYfe

Contents

Acknowledgements

I would like to sincerely thank the commissioning and editorial staff at The History Press for continuing to put their faith in my books and for the valuable advice and assistance they always provide. I would like to express my gratitude to my parents, my family, to Marcelline and my public support for continually pushing me to explore, think about and write about Cork city, its region and its cultural heritage.

For thirty years, Kieran has actively promoted Cork's heritage with its various communities and people. He has led and continues to lead successful heritage initiatives through his community talks, city school heritage programmes, walking tours, newspaper articles, books and his heritage consultancy business. For the past twenty-four years, Kieran has written a local heritage column in the *Cork Independent* on the history, geography and its intersection with modern-day life in communities in Cork city and county. Kieran is the author of thirty local history books. He holds a PhD in Geography from the National University of Ireland Cork and has interests in ideas of landscape, collective memory, narrative and identity structures. In June 2009, May 2014 and May 2019 Kieran was elected as a local government councillor (Independent) to Cork City Council. Kieran is Lord Mayor of Cork for 2023–24. He is also a member of the European Committee of the Regions. More on Kieran's work can be viewed at www.corkheritage.ie and www.kieranmccarthy.ie.

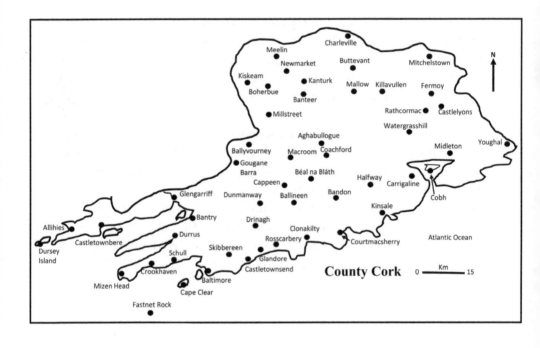

Introduction

'Curiouser and curiouser!' cried Alice in Lewis Carroll's *Alice's Adventures in Wonderland*. Such a famous literary phrase bounced around in my head as this book took shape. At the outset this book has been borne out of my own personal curiosity for many years now to venture off the main roads of County Cork to explore the 'wonderland' of cultural heritage in County Cork. Just like Alice's feeling of being lost, all too often I have felt lost on my scooter motorcycle in the county's precious winding and scenic roads. However, one is never truly lost in an age of Google Maps. But in any given day, I could be just a few kilometres from home and feel like being a grand explorer of a forgotten countryside.

The added task of picking over 100 curiosities of County Cork was also going to be a challenge. It is difficult to define what a curiosity is. Such a distinction varies from one person to another. The importance of a curiosity in one locale may not be a curiosity to another locale. The stories within this book, and which I have chosen and noted as curiosities, are ones that have lingered in my mind long after I found them or they brought me down further 'rabbit holes' of research.

Some curiosities are notable and well written about or some exist through a neighbourhood monument, a basic sign or a detailed information board showcasing they exist. Some are bound up with local folklore and referred to in a place name. Others could be deemed as strange events. However, all define the enduring sense of identity and place of a locale.

Being the largest county in Ireland, Cork has the advantage of also having the largest number of cultural heritage nuggets. However, with that accolade comes the conundrum of what nuggets to pick from. As with any A–Z of anything, it does not cover every single aspect of a particular history, but this book does provide brief insights into and showcases the nuggets and narratives of cultural interest that are really embedded in local areas. It also draws upon stories from across the county's geography.

Much has been written on the history of County Cork. There is much written down and lots more still to be researched and written up. The county is also blessed with active guardians of its past. In particular, there is a notable myriad of local historians and historical societies, which mind the county's past and also celebrate and commemorate it through penning stories in newspaper articles, journals, books and providing regular fieldtrips for the general public. There is also the impressive heritage book series on County Cork, published by the Heritage Unit of Cork County Council.

In addition, this book builds on *The Little Book of Cork* (2015) and *The Little Book of Cork Harbour* (2019), both History Press publications. It can be read in one go or dipped in and out of. I encourage you, though, once you have read it, to bring it out into the historic county of Cork to discover many of the curiosities up close and personal.

Enjoy, Kieran.

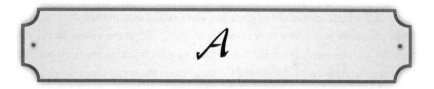

ABANDON

Just under 5km to the south-west of Macroom lies the Gearagh — a unique treasure trove of nature comprised of river channels flowing through an ancient forest system. Resulting from the flooding of an immense oak forest, a village and extensive farmland during the Lee Hydroelectric Scheme in the mid-1950s, the area is a miniature Florida swamp extending over 4.8km in length.

Annahala village was a little community with pockets of houses here and there. Some of the land had underlying limestone, which provided for fertile soil, while the rest of the land was boggy and marshy. At one time, Annahala had been an important lime-producing area with many lime kilns and a large population. Fuel for the kilns came from the Annahala bog, which had some very good turf banks, and timber from the Gearagh was also plentiful.

A *Cork Examiner* reporter visited the area on Friday, 26 October 1956, three days after the sluice gates of Carrigadrohid Dam had been closed. The reporter recorded the abandonment of the village in lamentful detail:

House in Annahala village, The Gearagh, Macroom, 28 October 1956. (*Irish Examiner*)

Some of the families had already left and were established in their new homes. Some are on the way. Some have nowhere to go! ... What trees there were have been cut and removed. From the flat terrain, newly created ruins stuck out like sore thumbs. As owners abandoned their cottages, slates and roofs were pulled off, and, in some cases, walls tumbled in. In one instance – that of the Gearagh's sole shop – only the concrete floor and foundations remain. But wisps of smoke still trickled from a few chimneys early yesterday.

Today, only the rectangular foundations of the houses survive amidst the undergrowth as well as the overgrown central small road through the village.

ANOMALY

(Rostellan Portal Dolmen)

To Cork and Irish archaeologists, the motives behind the building of the dolmen in Rostellan in north-east Cork Harbour is a mystery. It has three upright stones and a capstone, which at one time fell down but was later repositioned. It has a comparable design to portal tombs but this style of tombs is not familiar at all to this region of the country. For the visitor, the site is challenging to access. The beach on which it sits gets flooded at high tides and access across the local mudflats is tricky and dangerous. It is easier to get to it with a guide through the adjacent Rostellan wood. The dolmen may be a folly created by the O'Briens, former owners of the adjacent estate of Rostellan House, on whose estate an extensive wooded area existed. The house was built by William O'Brien (1694–1777), the 4th Earl of Inchiquin, in 1721.

ANTHEM

After the unsuccessful attempt at a rising in Ireland in March 1867, the principal participants, Colonel Thomas J. Kelly and Captain Timothy Deasy, two well-known Fenian leaders, emigrated to Manchester. They were arrested the following September.

Some of the Irish community in Manchester were determined to help them escape. However, the hold-up of the van while the prisoners were being transferred from Manchester to Salford Jail did not go according to plan. A shot fired through the lock in order to break it killed a policeman who was inside. The two prisoners escaped.

About thirty Irish people in Manchester were arrested on suspicion. Eventually, all were released except five. These were charged with wilful murder and sentenced to death. During the trial the condemned men started chanting the slogan 'God Save Ireland'. Three of the men were eventually taken to the gallows.

A few days after the executions, County Cork's well-known poet Timothy Daniel Sullivan wrote the words to a song and titled it 'God Save Ireland', weaving it with the air of an old song. Sullivan's song became so popular that later it was considered the Irish national anthem for a time.

Bantry-born Timothy Daniel Sullivan (1827–1914) began his career as an artist, then a journalist, obtaining a position on the staff of the *Nation* newspaper in 1854. He contributed many songs and articles to this paper. It was with simple ballads comprising themes of home and fatherland that he particularly excelled. He became editor and proprietor of the newspaper in 1876. Four years later, he became Nationalist member of Westminster Parliament for Westmeath, a seat he held until 1885 when he won the Dublin City constituency, which he represented until 1892. For the following eight years he was member for West Donegal.

APPARITION

On 22 July 1985, it was alleged a statue of the Virgin Mary in the grotto at Ballinspittle had moved. A local Garda saw the statue first move in July 1985 – and then photographed it. On dismissing the idea that he had a shake in his hand while taking a picture, he noted to the *Cork Examiner* that his camera was on a tripod, which held it perfectly steady. 'I took several pictures using a 80-200 Makinon zoom lens on this Olympus SLR camera. One picture showed the statue in its usual way but a follow-up picture taken from the same vantage point and without shaking the camera seems to show the arms in a different position.'

Events at the statue soon ensued. A local 100-person committee organised days of devotions. A bulldozer even worked long hours to prepare a 1-acre car park made available by a parishioner in a disused quarry midway between the village and the shrine. There were also toilets constructed by Cork County Council.

CIE – the national bus company – put on a number of bus services from the city and provincial towns. A number of private operators organised bus trips from many parts of the country. All roads within a mile of the shrine at each side were sealed off and pilgrims were advised to come well clad and to be prepared to stand for a long period. The crowds assembled on the slope opposite the shrine.

A serving sergeant in Cork city at the time saw the statue move two days after the first report in July 1985. He was among a crowd of several hundred people saying prayers and singing hymns in front of the grotto when suddenly, without warning, there was a gasp from the crowd as the statue, which is embedded in concrete, appeared to be airborne for half a minute. He noted: 'I was so convinced it was a fraud that I climbed up into the grotto the next morning and tried to shake the statue but it wouldn't budge. I checked the back, the sides of it for any trip wires, but I couldn't find anything.'

In the summer of 1985, over 100,000 people visited Ballinspittle in the hope of seeing the statue move. A spate of similar claims of moving statues occurred at about thirty locations across the country.

The advent of the nineteenth century coincided with the collection of folklore of the appearance of the Virgin Mary on the coastal side of Inchydoney Island near Clonakilty. Poet and story collector Joseph Callanan, in his works, *The Recluse of Inchidoney* (1829), tells of a local story of the Virgin Mary standing at one point in time on an elevated sand bank. According to folklore, she was discovered kneeling there by the crew of a vessel that was coming to anchor near the place. They sniggered at her and disrespected her, upon which a storm arose and devastated the ship and her crew. Attached to this tale is the 'Virgin Mary' shell story, about a fragile shell of the sea potato, a spined, urchin-like creature that burrows in the sand. It is told in the area still today that the 'M' shape of tiny perforations on the upper surface are said to denote Mary, the Mother of God, the dots indicating the number of beads of the Rosary, and, on the reverse side, some see the Sacred Heart.

APPOINTMENT

At one time, Elizabeth St Leger (1693/1695–1773/1775) of Doneraile House (later Mrs Aldworth) had the distinction of being the only female Freemason. Her appointment was more by accident than design. The North Cork Freemason's Lodge was held in Doneraile House in a room to the west of the entrance hall. Elizabeth was reading a book in an adjoining room, the back panel of which was under renovation and roughly put together. She fell asleep.

Elizabeth was awakened by hearing voices in the next room. Seeing a light through the spaces in the wall, she watched the proceedings of the Lodge.

Becoming alarmed, she attempted to escape but was challenged by Lord Doneraile's butler, who called His Lordship. Elizabeth was placed in the charge of some of the members while her case was deliberated upon by others. It was decided that the only way out of the difficulty was to make her a Freemason. She agreed, making her the first recorded female Freemason.

ARM

Saint Lachtin's Arm is a curious religious relic that was linked with Donoughmore Church. It is dated to *c.* 1120. It was created to sheathe a human bone, supposedly belonging to Saint Lachtin. For much of the medieval era, the guardians of the arm were the Healy family.

The shrine comprises a hollow core of yew wood and is about 400mm tall. Elaborate bronze panels with zoomorphic interlacing, highlighted with silver inlay, decorate the wooden core. Similar patterns can be viewed on the hand, which is cast in bronze. Unusually for hand shrines, the fist is clenched, which emphasises the hand's distinctive nails. The shrine carries writings, one of which is devoted to

St Lachtin's Arm relic on display at the National Museum, Dublin. (Kieran McCarthy)

its patron. This text reads: 'A prayer for Maolseachnail Ó Callaghan, Ard Rí of the Ua Ealach Mumhain who made this shrine'. Maolseachnail died in 1121. The arm is now on display in the National Museum, Dublin.

ASTRONOMICAL

Skibbereen-born Agnes Clerke can boast of having left a lasting legacy, not just on County Cork but on the universe. She had a crater on the Moon named after her in 1881. Clerke Crater lies at the edge of the Sea of Serenity.

Born in 1842, Agnes was sent to private education. Her family home in Skibbereen had a large library containing the classics in literature science, with technical equipment such as microscopes and telescopes and encyclopaedic connections from the world of nature. Agnes was attracted to the subject of astronomy through the influence of her father, John William, who mounted a 4in telescope in the family garden at night. Her mother influenced Agnes to be proficient in the rendition of old Irish airs on the harp and piano. By the time Agnes was 15 she had already written the first few chapters of her *History of Astronomy*.

Due to her delicate health, Agnes, with her mother and sister, spent at least six months of each year from 1867 to 1877 in Italy, in Naples, Rome or Florence. Agnes became fluent in several languages, including Italian, Latin, Greek, French and German.

In 1877, Agnes wrote an article during the height of the Sicilian Mafia, which was accepted for publication in the prestigious *Edinburgh Review*. Her writing was highly regarded and she became a regular contributor to the journal, penning over fifty articles, with many devoted to science and astronomy. Her book – *A Popular History of Astronomy During the Nineteenth Century* – was described by scientific writers as a masterpiece. From this came a nomination for a crater on the moon to be named after her.

In 1890, Agnes became a founder member of the British Astronomical Association, which provided facilities and organised events for anyone interested in astronomy. She went on to write book after book on all aspects of this branch of science.

AUTOPSY

On an information panel high up in Cousane Gap near Keakill, overlooking Bantry Bay, one encounters the story of body snatchers. In the early nineteenth century, bodies were dug up and robbed from the local cemetery in Kilmocomogue. They were for sale and use in anatomy classes in medical schools in Cork city to meet the necessity to carry out autopsies to study more about human anatomy and educate their students. It was legal for surgeons to dissect the bodies of convicted murderers, who were hanged for their crimes. But the small number of bodies handed over was not enough to meet the growing science of anatomy. A horse and cart conveyed the bodies from Kilmocomogue. However, the immoral activity was eventually targeted by a local vigilante group, who safeguarded freshly dug graves.

B

BEACON

Atop a cliff face, near Baltimore is the unique Baltimore Beacon, which provides a sweeping viewpoint over Baltimore Harbour and Sherkin Island. The striking conical, white-painted Baltimore Beacon, sometimes called the 'pillar of salt' or 'Lott's wife', is approximately 15.2m high and 4.6m in diameter at the base. Towards the end of July 1847, Commander James Wolfe, Royal Navy, notified the Ballast Board that he had recently completed a survey of Baltimore Harbour and observed the need for a beacon warning ships off the eastern point of the southern entrance to the harbour. It was over a year later, on 6 July 1848, before the Board invited the secretary to seek permission from Lord Carbery for a piece of ground 9.1m in diameter on which to build a new beacon.

BIRD

In the late summer of 1945, Professor Michael J. O'Kelly excavated sections of a ringfort in the townland of Garryduff on a small hill between Fermoy and Midleton. The fort was a small circular structure with a single rampart, which was first brought to notice when some shards of pottery were discovered by the landowner and were given to the professor. An excavation of the interior of the fort revealed several hearths, many postholes and some poorly preserved paved floors.

In an information report in the *Journal of the Cork Historical and Archaeological Society* in 1946, Professor O'Kelly outlines a beautiful and curious find. It was a small gold ornament which was in the form of a bird – a wren, to judge the bird's outline. The body had a beautiful pattern of scrollwork executed in beaded gold wire filigree. The object was constructed from a thin foil of gold beaten up into a convex form so as to give an impression of the roundness of the bird's body.

The dimensions of the object are extremely small – just 1.5cm. In other words, the whole bird is about the size of one little fingernail. One can only

Michael J. O'Kelly's picture of the Garryduff Bird. (Cork Public Museum)

admire all the more the high level of technical skill shown by the craftspeople who executed such work.

In a subsequent excavation report, published in 1963, Professor O'Kelly found no trace of military activity at the fort and concluded that the inhabitants of Garryduff were a peaceful but well-off community dedicated to their craftwork. Today, the bird piece can be viewed in Cork Public Museum.

BLACK

By the thirteenth century, the Celtic Church in Ireland was in decline. Across Europe, though, hundreds of thousands of young people were joining new and austere monastic orders, such as the Cistercians, Franciscans and Augustinians. Gaelic and Norman noblemen competed for the honour of being patron to the new religious orders. Alexander Fitzhugh, the Norman Lord of Castletownroche, created Bridgetown Priory in north Cork sometime between 1202 and 1216 for a community of Augustinian canons.

Up to 300 canons ended up living there and became known as the black canons because their habits (clothing) were black from head to toe. The canons were priests who had taken vows of poverty, obedience and chastity. They resided in the community according to the rule of St Augustine.

Fitzhugh gave the Augustinians 13 carucates of arable land, pasture and woodland, one third of his mills and fisheries and all tolls from the bridge that once stood there. Abbeys, priories, friaries and nunneries were soon established in Fermoy, Buttevant, Ballybeg, Glanworth and Castlelyons.

The priory prospered for over 200 years. At the time of its dissolution by King Henry VIII in 1541, its buildings, including a church with belfry, dormitory, hall, buttery, kitchen, cloister and cellar were all in ruins, its lands underpopulated and the property was worth less than £13. The buildings passed through almost a dozen landowners until it was taken over by Cork County Council.

In recent decades ongoing conservation work, facilitated by Cork County Council, on Bridgetown Priory has allowed the general public to explore the old ruins. Information panels reveal the secrets of the ruins and that the remains are substantially of the thirteenth century. They are among the most extensive of any religious house established in Ireland in that period.

BLOOD

In the parish of Durrus near Bantry lies Loch Na Fola, or Blood Lake. The 1937–38 National Schools Folklore Collection records that long ago, a man had to go to Durrus to fetch a priest for a sick person. He had to pass a place on the hill where a ghost was often seen. Near this place, there was a lake. He rode his horse to this location and took with him a scythe.

The man and his horse arrived at the point where the ghost was seen. Suddenly, his horse automatically halted. A ghostly tall man emerged from the landscape and strode before the horse on the road. The man raised his voice to the stranger, 'Come off the road and let the horse pass', but the ghost did not move. He reiterated his call several times, but the ghostly figure would not move from where he was.

The man grew angrier, dismounted his horse and cried, 'Are you going to come off the road and let the horse pass?' but the stranger did not stir. The man then struck him on the head with the scythe, which he had in his hand. The stranger fell to the ground and covered the whole place with blood. The man jumped on his horse and fled.

The blood steadily flowed into the adjacent lake, and in the morning it was overflowing with blood. Ever since, that lake has been called Loc Na Fola or, in English, Blood Lake.

BOWL

As a rich religious complex, it is easy to be curious about the pilgrimage traditions at St Gobnait's ruins in Ballyvourney. For example, touching St Gobnait's bowl three times forms part of the pattern of pilgrim acts.

The saint, through folklore, is represented as a woman of action. An invader of the area intended to construct a fortress on a hill near where the industrial estate is now located. St Gobnait's Hill overlooked the site and she threw an iron bowl at the structure, flattening it. The bowl returned to St Gobnait's hand, boomerang fashion.

Gobnait was also renowned as a beekeeper. The bees may well be considered her army. Rustlers were creating havoc in the district, stealing sheep and cattle, and the locals asked for Gobnait's help. She dispatched her bees on the trail and they routed the rustlers in a short time.

Gobnait is alleged to have been a native of the Aran Islands. In a vision, she was told to build her convent and church where she found nine white deer grazing. She travelled through Connacht and Munster in her quest. Many places in which she stayed are now known as 'Cill Ghobnait', or Kilgobnet. In Clondrohid, near Macroom, she saw some white deer, but not until she got to the townland of Gort na Tiobratan did she find exactly what she sought.

Since time immemorial, St Gobnait's Day, which is on 11 February, has been a local holiday. The saint's grave and marked spots are places where pilgrims pause for devotion and reflection. In addition, a medieval carved wooden statue is shown on her feast day at the local church, whereby ribbons are aligned the length of it. The ribbon is supposed to then be brought back to your home, where it can be used to ward off and cure sickness.

BRICK

One cannot but ponder on the tall, old chimney of Youghal Brickworks. It is such a recognisable landmark for travellers along the N25 Youghal bypass. Founded in 1895, in over a decade the Youghal Brick Company's factory was declared the most modern brick plant in the British Isles.

In 1913, the prestigious trade body, the British Brickmaker's Association, dispatched a delegation to Youghal Brickworks to examine the plant because of statements that a revolutionary technique of firing brick, which halved fuel consumption, was being successfully employed there. The claims were right – and the delegation duly reported back in very favourable terms to the *British Clayworker's Journal*.

It was manager J.R. Smyth who was responsible for progress. In Tony Breslin's thesis work on the brickworks, he outlines that Smyth was originally employed by H.R. Vaughan of Belfast, who owned the Laganville Brick Company. He was sent to Youghal to supervise the installation of a boiler bought from Laganville, and was invited to stay on to manage the newly incorporated Youghal Brick Company.

Soon after his arrival in 1896, J.R. arranged with a firm of German kiln constructors to build a Hoffman kiln. Invented by Frederick Hoffman in 1850, this was the first continuous-firing kiln and it had brought a new impetus to the

Corrin Cross and cairn, present day. (Kieran McCarthy)

brickmaking industry. It is the remains of this kiln, with its mighty chimney stack, which can be seen on the Youghal Brickworks site today – the only major structure now left of the entire complex.

The Hoffman was the most up-to-date kiln of the time. It became obsolete in less than fifteen years because it had a major drawback. It required a very tall chimney to draw down sufficient draught to operate properly. The performance of the kilns was thus, to some extent, dependent on the weather.

J.R. Smyth soon realised that the Hoffman, whatever advantages it had over earlier kilns, was still somewhat crude and wasteful. He therefore went to Germany, where kiln technology was more advanced than anywhere in the world, and he returned with new ideas. As a result, the Youghal Brick Company invested £3,000 in modernising the factory, including the installation of a revolutionary kiln designed by James Buhrer.

Between 1890 and 1920, the Youghal Brick Company was the leading Munster manufacturer and its products were used to build much of modern Cork. However, by 1929 it was all over. The Great Depression, the increase in coal prices and the rise of the concrete block became enormous economic obstacles.

BUCKET

The cairn atop Corrin Hill forest park overlooking Fermoy possibly may date to the early Bronze Age and it has been speculated that it is surrounded by a possible Iron Age hillfort. Local folklore relates an ancient story of a prince of the Fír Maigh Féine, who was cautioned by a Druid that his young son would perish in a drowning accident.

To thwart this foretelling, the prince instructed that a castle be constructed as far away from water as possible but at the highest peak in his kingdom. A great number of stones was carried to the peak of Corrin, while the lake at the base of the hill was drained. The latter feature became known as Ballyoran Bog or Currach na Druimmine ('marsh of the white-backed cow').

One day, while the great effort of conveying the building material to the site of the castle was continuing, the boy encountered an unattended bucket of water. Captivated by his own watery image, he fell into the bucket and drowned. The building of the castle was halted and never finished, leaving a cairn of stones at the top of the hill, where they still sit today. In 1933 an impressive large stone cross was erected next to the cairn.

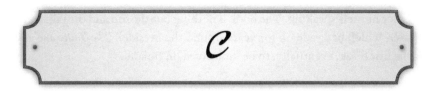

CENSOR

In 1941, the writer Eric Cross, fascinated by the vistas of Gougane Barra and the lives of its people, penned a series of articles in *The Bell* about two larger-than-life residents of Gougane, the Tailor, Tim Buckley, and his wife Ansty (Anastasia). Eric Cross was born in Newry, County Down, in 1905 and was educated as a chemical engineer. With no direct relationship with Tim Buckley and Ansty, he encountered the couple on a holiday to west Cork in the late 1930s or early 1940s. His interest in human nature brought him back to Gougane on several occasions and to interview the Tailor at length about his life.

The book – *The Tailor and Ansty* – was a result of Cross listening many nights to the Tailor's stories. It was published in 1942, and a hail of condemnation descended on Cross. The book was debated for four days in Seanad Éireann in 1943 after Sir John Keane tabled a motion condemning the censorship board for banning it. When Sir John Keane insisted on quoting from the book, one senator ordered the quotations to be stricken from the record in case 'pornographers might get their hands on them and peddle them in the marketplace'.

In a letter to the editor of the *Irish Press*, published on 15 October 1942 (p.3), Eric Cross defended the book:

> I wrote the book, *The Tailor and Ansty*, about a man who has been my friend for many years. The manuscript, before publication, was read by many other friends of the Tailor. When published it was received with gratitude by them and was reviewed enthusiastically by every Irish paper without any exception or objection. Last week the book was placed on the list of banned books by the Board of Censorship. Having stood the test of acceptance by the many of who are friends of the Tailor and the Press of Ireland. I must protest against the inference created by this ban.

In his introduction to the reprint of the book in 1964, Cork short story writer Frank O'Connor noted: 'Tis a funny state of affairs when you think of it. It is the Tailor himself speaking. The book is nothing but the fun and the talk and the laughter, which has gone on for years around the fireside.' *The Tailor and Ansty* was the first book, eventually, to be 'unbanned' in Ireland.

CHILDREN

Near the scenic village of Allihies in the Beara Peninsula is the curious and small white boulder site that according to folklore is where the children of Lir are buried. The story of the children is a famous legend in Ireland. Indeed, there are many areas in Ireland that allege to be the landing spot of the swans after their 900-year journey on the seas and lakes of Ireland.

A sign posted by Beara Tourism relates the myth of a jealous stepmother and her banishment of her stepchildren to roam as swans for 900 years:

> The children were the sons and daughters of Lir, a member of the Tuatha de Danaan clan, who married Eve daughter of King Bov the Red, King of the Tuatha de Danaan. Eve and Lir were blissfully married and had a set of twins – Aed and Finola, and after a short period there followed another set of twins, 2 boys, Conn and Fiara. Unfortunately, Eve died soon after and Lir, not wanting his children growing up without the love of a mother, married Eva, King Bov's second daughter. This was a happy marriage until Eva became jealous of Lir's devotion of his children.
>
> Overcome with hatred she brought the children to Lough Darravagh near their home and transformed them into swans. Realising what she had done and overcome with remorse, she attempted to release the spell but could only ease their distress by enabling them to speak and sing and to remain as swans for 900 years until Christianity was introduced into Ireland. The swans spent the first 300 years on Lough Darravagh close to their home. The next 300 years was spent on the Sea of Moyle, a cold and desolate area between Scotland and the north of Ireland. The last 300 years they endured on the Atlantic sea.
>
> When their time was over the swans, attracted by the ringing of a bell rung by a monk living in Allihies village in the Beara Peninsula, came ashore and immediately were changed back into their human form. The children were by now old men and women (and) were baptised by the monk. A short time later they died and were buried under these large white boulders.

Pilgrimage rounds are still made by the local people circling the boulders. Money is still placed on and under the boulders as an offering to the children.

Children of Lir Boulder site, Allihies, present day. (Kieran McCarthy)

CLAPPER

Adjacent to the village of Ballingeary, a part of which sits upon the course of the River Lee, is a structure known as a clapper bridge. The name is derived from the Anglo-Saxon word '*cleaca*', which means 'bridging the stepping stones'.

The Ballingeary example is one of a few that are the longest of their type in Ireland. However, there is scarce information as to when the bridge was initially built, although it was possibly inspired by more ancient bridges along the river, which are long gone. It is shown on a first edition Ordnance Survey map of *c*.1840.

There are five protected clapper bridges in County Cork. Three bridges of this type may be viewed in the area. This one is the best preserved and most striking with its length of 145m, even running into the adjacent field.

An adjacent information panel relates that for many years, the clapper bridge has withstood the force of floods of the River Lee. Its shape in the form of a curve has helped in maintaining its structural integrity. The sign reads: 'The bridge is

Clapper bridge at Ballingeary, present day. (Kieran McCarthy)

curved upstream towards the flow of the river. The greater the flow the tighter and stronger the bridge becomes. There was no mortar or concrete used in its construction … Downstream, in the centre, there is an island, which prevents eddy currents from undermining the bridge.'

The stones of the bridge themselves are large slabs, which would have had to be transported there from a distance. The longest one in the centre has a 2.3m span.

CLOAK

Cloaks were and still are synonymous with west Cork; it was a wool outer garment worn for many centuries. Thomas Crofton Croker, in his book entitled *Researches in the South of Ireland* (1824), under his 'Manners and Customs' chapter describes that in the eastern baronies of County Cork and County Limerick, cloaks of the brightest red could be seen. In the west of Cork and Kerry, dark blue and grey prevailed. Previous to the Irish Rebellion of 1798, the former colour was more commonly worn but since the increase in policing due to insurrection, and hence the presence of the British redcoat, the colour red became generally disused.

Croker describes the importance of the cloak:

> The cloak is a part of dress apparently never superfluous to an Irish woman and is constantly used with the hood over the head, even during the hottest days of summer; those who are not so fortunate as to possess a cloak turn the skirt of their gown or an apron over their shoulders, and in this huddled style proceed about their out-door occupations with as little alacrity as might be expected.

There was also a strong desire to possess a pair of silver buckles or a silver clasp for the cloak – such features were handed down from mother to daughter with the greatest care as family heirlooms.

In an exhibition in the Michael Collins Centre in Clonakilty, the research outlines that by the early twentieth century, the use of hooded cloaks had died out in most parts of Ireland except west Cork. Dressmakers in and around towns like Clonakilty, Skibbereen, Kinsale, Bandon and Bantry kept on the tradition of making the black cloaks. While the basic design was the same there were differences in the cloaks, such as different beaded braids which were arranged by the cloak makers.

The cloaks had an important role during the Irish War of Independence when they were used to hide weapons. In Bandon they were worn up until recently but today they are seen only during celebrations and festivities.

COLONY

Usually resting on local rocks, the seal colony, which can be observed en route by ferry to Garinish Island, Glengarriff, is one of the best seal watching locations in County Cork and the whole of Ireland. At any one time, over 250 harbour seals (*Phoca vitulina* and also known as the common seal) can be viewed.

Ireland's National Parks and Wildlife Service records the scene as a special area of conservation and regularly monitors the location. The Service in its conservation report records that the harbour seals in Glengarriff Harbour occupy both aquatic habitats and intertidal shorelines that become exposed in the course of the tidal cycle. The harbour seal is a flourishing aquatic predator that feeds on a wide array of fish, cephalopod and crustacean species. The report notes of the life cycle of a seal:

> For individual harbour seals, of all ages, intervals between foraging trips in coastal or offshore waters are spent resting ashore at terrestrial or intertidal haul-out sites, or in the water … The species is present at the site throughout the year during all phases of its annual life cycle which includes breeding (May to July approximately), moulting (August to September approximately) and non-breeding foraging and resting phases.

COMMUNE

Off the beaten track, near Leap in west Cork is the townland of Clounkeen, where there is an elaborate memorial plaque to William Thompson (1775–1833) and to his ideas of a commune for the local area. Thompson was a pioneer of socialism, women's rights, workers' rights and tenants' rights when these concepts were very novel indeed.

At the unveiling of the memorial in September 2001, Michael Tobin of Rosscarbery Historical Society gave a detailed account of his life and times. Born in Cork city, it seems that William Thompson was self-educated. He was well read in both French and English. He studied the texts of the socialist philosophers in Europe. He tried to apply the teachings of the French and other continental socialists and philosophers to relieve the extreme poverty of the people here, who were exploited by unjust and corrupt landlords.

William was 39 years old when he inherited his Leap estate. He was not an absentee landlord. Between 1824 and 1830 he wrote four major books in his specially constructed turret. His fourth and final book was about the Co-operative movement, which was written in 1830. William had plans to begin a Co-operative Community in Carhoogarriff, and in his will he bequeathed his property to thirteen trustees to apply to co-operative purposes.

According to local tradition, William had laid the foundation of his community centre in Carhoogarriff. He had prepared a draft constitution of his own community. It offered the complete freedom of thought and expression on all subjects without regard for the feelings of others. Religion was to be a private concern. Women were to be entitled to advance to all political offices and jobs.

In 1833 William died before his ambitious plans could be completed. In time his works were studied by Karl Marx during research for *Das Kapital*. He was described by James Connolly as the 'first Irish socialist'.

It was over sixty years after William's death, in 1894, that Horace Plunkett founded the farming co-operatives. These co-operatives were well managed, and they kept this country going during the difficult years of the 1920s, '30s, '40s and '50s. A short distance from the Thompson memorial is the successful Drinagh Co-op, which was founded in 1923.

COUSINS

Cousins Edith Somerville (1858–1949) and Violet Martin Ross (1862–1915) are best known as 'Somerville and Ross', authors of the much-loved 'Irish RM' stories. Violet, born in Galway in 1862, was four years Edith's junior. They met each other for the first time at the Somerville home in Castletownshend in 1886. Within a year the cousins were inseparable. Edith always called Violet by the name 'Martin' – it prevented misunderstanding with other family members who shared her Christian name. Edith and Martin originally commenced writing to entertain themselves, but they amazed their family when their first effort at fiction – *An Irish Cousin* – was published by Bentleys in 1889.

For over ten years, Edith turned down regular proposals of marriage from Herbert Greene, an Oxford don. He finally gave up. At the age of 22, Edith had promised herself that she would earn her own living, and this more or less precluded marriage.

Both Edith and Violet stayed unmarried and revelled in the freedom that this granted them as they journeyed all over Europe penning novels and stories. The fame of the 'Irish RM' stories was essentially due to their hunting interests. Both Somerville and Ross were avid hunters, with Edith becoming the first woman Master of Foxhounds in Ireland. Their great expertise of horses, and their love of the chase, won them the respect of their male readership.

Apart from their careers as writers, both women committed their lives and the majority of their incomes to providing family homes that they could never hope to inherit. Violet expended much time refurbishing the family home at Ross, County Galway, while Edith managed the family farm with her sister Hildegarde. Edith bought, trained and sold horses in America and England, and she and her pioneered the introduction of the first herd of pedigree Friesian cattle to Ireland.

As committed feminists, they were founding members of the Munster Women's Franchise League. After Violet was seriously injured in a bad hunting fall in 1898, Edith dedicated much time to looking after her. In December 1915, as Violet lay dying in the Glen Vera nursing home in Cork, Edith remained by Violet's bedside until her death on 21 December.

After Violet's death, Edith continued to write under both their names. She wrote a further six novels, convinced of Martin's heavenly assistance. The partnership turned out thirty-two novels. Edith herself died in 1949. The cousins are buried alongside each other in St Barrahane's graveyard in Castletownshend.

DAIRY

In the late nineteenth century, the Gates brothers, from Guildford, Surrey, owned the West Surrey Dairy Company, which produced Britain's first powdered milk and became a major baby food manufacturer.

One of them, William Gates, founded the Gates Creamery at Kildorrey in north Cork in 1887. The company's creameries used the latest separating and drying equipment for the production of cream. The Kildorrey cream factory was acknowledged as the first of its kind in Ireland. William was considered as one of the country's leading dairy experts. In addition, he was a qualified dentist, and operated a very successful practice in Kildorrey.

In 1891, a trademark logo was developed and adopted of a cow looking through a farm gate.

Initially, cream was the main product at Kildorrey and as a by-product of cream production, milk powder was produced for use as a baking ingredient. In 1904, an article was published by the Carnegie Institute in the US, highlighting the strong health benefits detected after feeding children with milk powder. The medical profession instantly adopted this new concept and the infant nutrition business commenced.

In 1929, the Gates-owned company became Cow & Gate. The Kildorrey creamery continued to play a key role in the economic and social life of the area. In 1947 the manufacturing operation transferred to Mallow and from there its milk products were exported around the world.

Due to the rising need, a plan of expansion was embarked on and in the early 1970s the company financed a brand new plant in Wexford. Since then, Cow & Gate has gone from strength to strength, now employing 350 people in its facilities in Macroom and Wexford town.

Today, the site of the first Gates Creamery has a beautiful limestone plaque sculpted by Ken Thompson.

DEATH

Three Castle Head is truly an epic location. It is said that the O'Donoghues, who were the last family to live there, all died by suicide or murder. Now, as a result, a drop of blood falls from one of the towers every day. Others claim that a mysterious lady in white haunts the lake and anyone who sees her will die soon after.

Situated on a western headland above the Mizen Head, Dun Locha or Dunlough, or Fort of the Lake, sits atop the brink of a 100m cliff face on the site of an ancient promontory fort. In its day, it was an crucial tactical position with 360-degree views of the landscape.

Historical information signs on the approach to the castle tell of an annal record that it was built by Donagh na Aimrice O'Mahoney, Donagh the Migratory, in 1207. He is alleged to be a scholar and traveller on pilgrimages to the Holy Land. Irish archaeologists have noted that the extant ruinous towers with their curtain walls are more fifteenth century in date and possibly were added to an earlier structure.

Three Castle Head, present day. (Kieran McCarthy)

DESTRUCTION

As the Irish War of Independence progressed in the early summer of 1920, tensions escalated and violence ensued between the Irish Republican Army (IRA) and British forces. One additional element of force, which appears more and more in witness statements and across the newspapers of 1920, was the use of arson. It was used on both sides of the conflict, especially in the destruction of buildings. It was an aspect that also culminated in the Burning of Cork in December 1920.

In May 1920, the burning of old landed estate, Big Houses, by the IRA began and intensified as the War of Independence progressed. Historian James Donnelly, in a journal article in *Éire-Ireland* in 2012, records that burnings of such houses were a common occurrence in County Cork but were rare outside of the county. Fifty Big Houses and suburban villas were burned there before the Truce in July 1921. Forty of the fifty structures were burned throughout Cork from April 1921 until the Truce on 11 July 1921.

On early Tuesday morning, 25 May 1920, Kilbrittain Castle, a historic Big House style of mansion, 11km from Bandon and standing on an eminence overlooking a most scenic spot, was destroyed by arson. IRA volunteers were determined to prevent the occupation of the mansions in question by the British military or police forces or sought to punish their owners for allowing or encouraging such use. The IRA's first burning of a Cork Big House was certain to seize public attention because of the sheer size, prominence and opulence of the Kilbrittain Castle mansion. The damage was estimated at least £100,000.

Brigade Staff Officer and member of Cork No. 3 Brigade, Michael Crowley, in his witness statement now held in the Bureau of Military History (no. WS 1603), records that by April and May 1920, his battalion were continually endeavouring to locate Royal Irish Constabulary patrols, which usually patrolled the countryside for some miles around their barracks. Despite being on the RIC's most wanted list, they continued to engage and disarm RIC members. However, by August 1920 in the overall picture of County Cork as many as eight infantry battalions (20 per cent of the total) and one cavalry regiment were stationed in the county or city of Cork alone. The historical tensions had been replaced with all-out war.

DISEASE

Disease was a major cause of death during the Irish Great Famine (1845–49). People were exhausted by hunger. They were very vulnerable to illness, which was easily distributed by overcrowded conditions and the large movement of famine victims. Doctors fought to cope with a wide range of diseases, many of which were lethal. The correlation between famine and disease was not fully recognised and medical knowledge and resources lacked in the midst of such a large-scale calamity.

The term 'famine fever' generally refers to two of the most serious diseases – relapsing fever and typhus. Other serious illnesses consisted of dysentery, smallpox, Asiatic cholera, famine dropsy, measles, scarlatina and consumption.

The elaborate exhibition on the Great Famine in Skibbereen Heritage Centre relates that in the town's Abbeystrewery Graveyard lie an estimated 8,000 to 10,000 famine victims who died of starvation and disease. Countless people buried their dead covertly by night, too ashamed to be seen doing so without a coffin or shroud, or too scared to have it known that fever had entered their dwelling. One tale tells of a farmer burying his wife in the graveyard under cover of darkness and meeting their two close neighbours who were burying their brother. Until that moment the farmer and his neighbours had been unaware of each other's bereavement.

DITCH

The Cliadh Dubh, or the Black Ditch, runs for over 13.5 miles from the Ballyhoura Mountains to the Nagle Mountains. This ancient linear earthwork, which is estimated at over 1,000 years old, crosses the Blackwater Valley in north-east County Cork.

Dovecote at Cronody townland, River Lee Valley, present day. (Kieran McCarthy)

Rich folklore presents many tales on the origins of the ditch. One tale relates that a huge black boar with large tusks angrily tore through the countryside leaving a vast earthen linear mound. Another tale speaks of a large worm burrowing its way through the land.

However, the real reason for its construction and its use will never be known. Among the more plausible reasons is that it could define an ancient territorial border and help defend important paths and routeways, or even protect cattle from attacks from wild animals or from other people's raids. Comparable earthworks can be discovered in other parts of Ireland – for example, the Black Pig's Dyke, which shaped the margins of the ancient Kingdom of Ulster.

In the present day, the Cliadh Dubh is mostly difficult to recognise within its immediate landscape and field boundaries. However, it still provides boundaries for several townlands and parishes.

DOVE

Cronodymore House, just south of Dripsey in the River Lee Valley, was of a rectangular plan, 18.3m long in the front facing south and 7.6m deep. It was three storeys high with a chimney standing up at each of the four corners of the structure. The site appears on the Ordnance Survey map of the area in 1844 (Sheet No. 72). The building was a roomy structure for its day. The current structure was built over 100 years ago, more or less on the site of the previous house.

Cronody also bears the native addition of *Coradh-noide-na-n-abhall-milish*, i.e. 'Cronody of the sweet apples'. Apple trees at one time abounded all over the townland. Perhaps the most notable structure in Cronody today and an unusual feature in the Lee Valley is a dovecote, or pigeon house. Overlooking the reservoir and in very good condition, it is a roofless and circular stone-built structure. The building was weather-slated on the outside.

The dovecote has been dated to *c.*1716, the same time Cronody House was erected. Measuring about 5m in diameter and 6 to 7m in height, the entrance of the dovecote has a round-headed door opening on the southern side. The masonry of the interior walls is random rubble and comprises slabs of sandstone carefully built upon each other. A collection of fifteen rows of nesting boxes can be seen. In Herbert Webb Gillman's article on Cronody in 1895 in the *Journal of the Cork Historical and Archaeological Society*, he noted that each row contained thirty holes, making 450 nests in all.

The nests are in the shape of an L. Each nest entrance is large enough to put in your arm. The bend in the L gave good shelter for the nest. Gillman observed that the nests were visited twice a month for the young birds, and pigeon pies must have formed some of the dishes provided by the residents of Cronody for its guests.

In the latter half of the nineteenth century the owner of Cronodymore kept a superior breed of carrier pigeons. Those that were trained and put into use had a small silver label each on their neck. They were used for bringing news of racing events from England. Mr Ford of Dripsey village told the story to Mr Gillman of the long distances that those birds travelled. They bore news in the time of Ford's great-grandfather, who was interested in horse racing events. Doncaster in Yorkshire is mentioned as one of the points from which the birds started.

✳ ✳ ✳

Another notable dovecote is at the ruinous Ballybeg Abbey near Buttevant. There is also a well-preserved columbarium with a corbelled roof and more than 300 roosts. In 1229 Philip de Barry endowed the Priory of Ballybeg for regular canons following the rule of St Augustine and in remembrance of his endowment his equestrian statue in brass was erected in the church. Visitors can view the remains of the church, three-storey tower and stone coffins.

DUPLICATE

St Luke's Church in Cork city opened for worship in 1837 as a chapel of ease to St Anne's Church, Shandon. In 1872, St Luke's became a separate parish and it was decided to rebuild the church to provide more extensive accommodation.

The spire was purchased for the sum of £100 by the Very Rev. Canon Holland, Parish Priest of Innishannon, for erection in the Roman Catholic church. Stone by stone, it was taken down and brought the 26km to its present prominent position overlooking Innishannon village and the River Bandon. The work of its re-erection commenced in June 1875 and was completed in June 1876.

The new parish church of St Luke's, which was finished in 1875, had a short life because it was completely destroyed by fire twelve years later (in 1887). Immediately, however, the work of building the present beautiful church commenced. This was completed within two years and the modern St Luke's Church (and now a concert venue) was opened for service in 1889.

EARS

In the centre of Lough Hyne, located just outside Skibbereen, there is an island and on its eastern side stand the ruins of Labhra Ó Leencha's castle. It is reputed that the chieftain who lived there had two ears as large as those of a donkey.

Eibhlín Ní Chárthaigh from Clochar na Trócaire (Convent of Mercy), in her Schools' Folklore Collection file from about 1937 38, outlines the legend in broader detail using what she picked up from chatting to locals. The chieftain who lived there was so adamant about concealing his ears that he often engaged in murder. Once in twelve months he got his hair cut and the lot fell on one of the neighbours to cut it.

Eibhlín's account outlines that it happened at one time that the lot fell on a widow's only son and it was also known that the barber would be put to death lest he should betray the secret:

> The widow pleaded so earnestly with the King that her son was allowed to live on condition that he would never reveal the secret to anybody. The boy was ailing and he went to a priest and told him he had a secret which he could not let out. Then the priest told to dig a sod and tell the secret to the ground and the boy carried out his order. The sod was dug near the shore of a lake and when the reeds grew up and the first gust of wind blew them, they commenced to sing 'Tá dhá chluais capaill ag Labhar Ó Loingsigh' or 'Labhar Ó Loingsigh has two donkey ears'. So when the king heard this he took his boat and was last seen sailing over the ocean.

Another version of the above is that the boy went to a Druid for advice and was told to ease his mind by telling the secret to a hazel tree. Later, a harper made a harp from the wood and the instrument could be got to play nothing but the refrain '*Tá dhá chluais capaill ag Labhar Ó Loingsigh*'.

ENRICH

In the townland of Ard na Gaoithe, near Watergrasshill in mid-County Cork, adjacent the local ancient church and graveyard lie the accessible but ruined and curious remains of a lime kiln. It is one of hundreds scattered across County Cork and across the Irish landscape. Their curiosity lies in their function for enriching the land with powdered lime as fertiliser.

The powder was created by burning limestone rocks in an enclosed kiln. Where limestone was an underlining rock, it was readily accessible. Limestone was initially smashed up into smaller pieces. They were put in the kiln from the top with alternate layers of existing fuel such as oak or turf.

Burning lime involved an immense volume of work: digging or constructing the kiln, collecting rocks, chopping, carting and throwing fuel down the kiln, keeping attention on the kiln. The kiln was lit and burned for up to a fortnight before the fire was permitted to be extinguished. After a cooling period, the burnt limestone was withdrawn through an opening at the base. Water was spread over the burnt stone, and it slaked off into hydrated or slaked lime.

Lime kiln at Ard na Gaoithe townland, Watergrasshill, with locals Kyle Furney Kelly, Fia Furney Kelly and Ned Quigley, December 2022. (Kieran McCarthy)

Burnt lime had a wide range of functions. Lime mortar could be used for fertiliser and bonding stone walls, as well as providing limewash for painting traditional-style Irish cottages. Lime could be used for softening water and decreasing the acidity of butter, cream, milk and 'sour' soil. Other applications include sanitising outhouses and making sheep dip, drying cuts on livestock, tanning leather and killing insect pests.

ENTREPRENEUR

Born in 1866 into Coolbane Mills, Freemount, near Kanturk, County Cork, Andrew O'Shaughnessy was the second son of Andrew and Ellen O'Shaughnessy. In a lecture later in life, Andrew Junior eloquently put it that, 'I was born within the sound of the mill wheel.' His father died when he was 15 and he was asked to help with the mill in Freemount. The mill was one of five O'Shaughnessy mills in north Cork. He decided to emigrate to America and spent several months there. He came back to Ireland but shortly went back again to the States again to attend business school in New York. He spent his 21st birthday in the 'Big Apple'. America in those years produced very talented inventors like Thomas Edison and his electric light bulb, whilst other great minds – such as Alexander Graham Bell – also took their ideas overseas.

Andrew was described in later years as a man of vision and foresight, traits that were forged during his stay in America. After absorbing some American business and manufacturing ideas, he came home and rented an old mill, which he converted into a creamery at Newmarket in 1895. He soon added six more central creameries at Mitchelstown, Coachford and Knockulty and Mullinahane in County Tipperary. He also established twenty-four branches of his Newmarket concern, thereby creating a chain under the name of the Newmarket Dairy Company in 1904. In the ensuing years, Andrew added Bridgetown Flour Mills, Sallybrook Woollen Mills, Kilkenny Woollen Mills and Dripsey Woollen Mills to his operation.

In 1922, the number employed at Dripsey Woollen Mills was sixty and the mill had fourteen looms and three carding machines as well as a plant to produce its own electricity.

In 1982, an article in the *Cork Examiner* by Evelyn Ring on 12 April 1982 charted the decline of woollen mills. There was a continuing contraction of the milling craft, particularly within the European Economic Community. In 1982, there were forty-five men and twenty-five women employed at Dripsey

Woollen Mills, but in 1988 the mills were sold off and bought by a receiver. Today, what are left are just the memories. The main building is demolished. Ruinous sheds now stand without their roofs.

EXHIBITIONIST

High up on the eastern wall at Ballinacarriga Tower House, near Dunmanway in west Cork, is a sheela-na-gig. It is difficult to view on the wall. The figure has a big nose and big right ear. Her legs are short. Her right hand passes behind her right leg, the left hand passes in front of the left leg and both hands keep her vulva wide open as a display of female genitalia.

Sheela-na-gigs are regarded as both erotic symbols to avert evil or of fertility, or even to highlight the dangers of sexual promiscuousness. Some are even seen as obscene. Their exact purpose is unknown, which is what makes them a fascinating subject to explore. Such female exhibitionist carvings are found throughout the country's ancient church and castle buildings. Many have been vandalised, disappeared or moved. They date from the eleventh and thirteenth centuries but it seems their status in Ireland continued well into the seventeenth century.

The sheela-na-gig at Ballinacarriga Tower House would have had to be placed there by the Hurley family. There may be a connection to the marriage of Randal Hurley to Catherine Cullinane in 1585. Their marriage is commemorated on the inside of one of the fourth-storey windows.

One can see two more sheela-na gigs up close at Cork Public Museum, where there is one from Tracton Abbey and one from Ringaskiddy on display.

EXPEDITION

Cork-born Edward Bransfield was born in 1785 to an influential Catholic seafaring family in the port town of Ballinacurra, near Midleton. In 1803, when a British warship docked at Youghal Harbour, 18-year-old Edward enlisted in the service of the Royal Navy. He had some maritime training from his father, who owned and traded with his own boat. Despite the blitz of death during the Napoleonic Wars, he survived. Edward climbed quickly through the naval ranks – first to the status of an officer and finally attaining the rank of ship's master.

When the war ended in 1815, Edward Bransfield took up a position in the navy's new Pacific Squadron in Valparaiso, Chile. While there, in 1819, a British merchant ship named the *Williams* made port detailing that it had viewed uncharted lands south of Cape Horn. Edward was sent to explore the account. He commandeered the *Williams* and led a crew of thirty men. They sailed 3,200km south from Valparaiso in December 1819. On 20 January 1820, Bransfield glimpsed 'two high mountains, covered in snow'. He had discovered what is now called the Trinity Peninsula, the northernmost point of the Antarctic continent.

Today, in honour of his exploration work, Edward Bransfield is remembered through a number of named Antarctica landmarks: Bransfield Island, Bransfield Trough, Bransfield Rocks, Mount Bransfield and the Bransfield Strait. In 2000, Edward Bransfield was recognised for his discovery when the British Royal Mail issued a stamp in his honour. As no likeness of the man has survived, the stamp portrayed an image of RRS *Bransfield*, a British Antarctic surveying vessel.

In 2020, a beautiful monument by sculptor Matthew Thompson was unveiled at the entrance to Ballinacurra village. A limestone base was then designed by the committee, including the names of other Irish Antarctic explorers surrounding the monument, and Matthew's monument sits on a map of the Antarctic.

EXPENSIVE

St Colman's Cathedral was completed in 1919 for a total cost of £235,000. It far exceeded its initial proposed cost. It was the most expensive single building constructed in Ireland in the late nineteenth and early twentieth centuries. On 24 August 1919, impressive ceremonies took place at Queenstown (now Cobh) to consecrate St Colman's Cathedral. Local newspapers such as the *Cork Examiner* covered the event and the cathedral history was well documented in its August 1919 spread. Since then many historians, locally and internationally, have written on the gorgeous building and its impressive over 90m tall spire.

The building of a cathedral in Queenstown was the conception of Dr William Keane, Bishop of Cloyne from 1857 to January 1874. He had personal knowledge of the grand Gothic cathedrals of France, where he had lived for the greater part of his life as a student and Superior in the Irish College, Paris. The cathedral is one of Edward W. Pugin and George Ashlin's most important Irish commissions. It is one of the finest examples of ecclesiastical architecture in the Gothic revival style in Ireland.

FAMILY

Dating from the early seventeenth century in the south transepts of St Mary's Collegiate Church, Youghal, lies the Boyle Chapel. Here one can view the elaborate family monument erected by Richard Boyle (*c.*1602–43) in his own and family's honour. Richard Boyle was an entrepreneur from Canterbury who became one of the most powerful characters in Britain and Ireland during the early seventeenth century.

In December 1601, Walter Raleigh sold his 42,000-acre Irish estate to Richard Boyle for the paltry sum of £1,500. The purchase included the towns of Youghal, Cappoquin and Lismore, all linked by the navigable River Blackwater, as well as castles, lands and fisheries, with the extra bonus of the ship called *Pilgrim*. Temple Michael, Molana Abbey and the parkland at Ballynatray were also now given over to Boyle. He had a substantial residence, known today as The College, close to St Mary's Collegiate Church.

In time, Boyle's main estates were in counties Cork and Waterford but he also owned significant property in County Kerry, including lands in the baronies of Corkaguiny and Dunkerron South. In the early seventeenth-century maps of Munster, some of the key settlements that Boyle was involved in creating appear. In time, many of these developed into well-loved and beautiful County Cork towns – for example, Bandon and Clonakilty, both of which underpin west Cork's regional heritage and identity.

The monument rests on a high plinth, or stylobate, divided into a centre and wings. The latter are sculptured in bas relief with inverted torches, crossbones and swords in saltier. Above them rise Ionic, Composite and Corinthian columns of different-coloured marbles, with their entablatures, receding in gradation until they terminate, nearly at the full height of the building, in an obelisk standing on four balls.

Obelisks likewise crown the lower parts of the monument. An ornamented arched recess over the plinth contains the recumbent effigy of the earl, exceedingly well executed. He is represented in a suit of engraved russet and gold armour of the reign of James I. It has double tassets and is richly ornamented throughout. His head is uncovered, the face gazing heavenward, and from the position of the monument, looking to the east, he leans on his left hand supported by a cushion; while, as Lord High Treasurer of Ireland, he holds in his right hand his purse of office. Over his shoulders and his armour are capes or lappets of an earl's mantle of state, which hangs down behind his feet. Underneath, along the edge of the plinth, are nine small figures (now much broken) representing the children that were born to him up to the date of the erection of the monument, i.e. 1619.

At the earl's feet, under a canopy supported by Ionic pillars of red-veined marble, kneeling on a tasselled cushion, with hands folded in prayer, is the figure of his first wife, Joan, daughter and co-heir of William Appsley, Esq., of Limerick. Her dress is of the richest figured satin, and a dark purple mantle hangs behind her back. Under a corresponding canopy, at the earl's head, and in the

Boyle family memorial at St Mary's Church, Youghal, present day. (Kieran McCarthy)

same posture, is the effigy of his second wife, Katherine, only daughter of Sir Geoffry Fenton, principal Secretary of State for Ireland. She wears a countess's robe of state in rich crimson, paling Boyle with their arms, respectively. Over the arch is the recumbent effigy of the earl's mother, Joan.

FERRY

For many decades up to 1923, a manually operated ferry popularly described as a pontoon-type bridge made five or six trips daily across East Ferry – across the eastern channel off Great Island to the general Rostellan area. The old Irish name of the ferry was Caladh Ratha, or the Ferry of the Rath (ringfort). The rath, or *lios*, was situated near the ferry point on the Great Island. It transported passengers, carts and cattle from shore to shore. Old and rare pictures show two pontoons arranged catamaran-like, decked over and fitted at either end with a landing ramp. The pontoon was chain-hauled between its two terminals of sorts and served a great social need. Information regarding its end is conflicting. It was targeted and rendered inoperative during the Irish Civil War but to what extent it was rebooted is hazy and not recorded. Local boating still exists in the area and despite the fact the ferry does not run any more, the licence is renewed for heritage reasons every year.

FISH

In July 1630, Sir Thomas Butlin noted that the walled town of Kinsale 'stands where the greatest fishing is of herring, hake and salmon, and where the greatest provision is made of fishing, for all the western parts of any port in the West of Ireland'. Kinsale Harbour had an abundant supply of fish which, over time in the seventeenth century, became a major factor in the initial development of a profitable fishing industry. Even though fish was abundant, the law at the time stated that the sovereign in Kinsale had permission to take the best, which included haddock, cod, ling, halibut and other small types.

The summer of 1790 coincided with the arrival of Charles Etienne Coquerbert de Montbret, a Frenchman, to Kinsale. He was on holiday, travelling around and exploring Munster. He stated that it was the fishing industry more than the foreign trade that Kinsale drew its wealth from. Such was the abundance of fish that ray were even dumped by the local fishermen.

Fast forward to over a century later, in 1880. On reviewing the enormous fishing trade of the port, the Harbour Commissioners decided to build a large pier that would encompass all other small piers in the south-eastern section of the town. The full cost of the pier, which included the purchase of land and private rights, amounted to £18,050, and this was to be funded by the Board of Works loan and a town treasury grant.

By pure coincidence, by the time the pier was fully functional at the turn of the 1900s, Kinsale's greatest economic asset, the fishing industry, began to decline. Several reasons have been put forward by historians why this decline occurred.

Vast shoals of mackerel off Kinsale Harbour went westwards. Rival coastal towns such as Glandore, Castletownsend, Baltimore and Berehaven took advantage of this situation and developed their own fishing industries. The new fishing stations set up in the south-west were soon to outdistance and outlive Kinsale's fishing industry. There was also a discovery of new shoals of mackerel off the western shores of England, which meant that English boats now remained in their home territory. The increasing use of steam as the principal movement agent in fishing boats became a strong factor in the decay of Kinsale's fishing industry. No longer did fishing boats, especially English ones, sail into an Irish port when on the Irish Sea; it was easier and faster to use steam to go back to England.

Following years of economic decay, in 1958, deep sea angling, especially for blue sharks, was investigated as a potential profit maker for the town. In 1960, a group of businessmen, with financial help from Bord Fáilte (the Irish tourism board) established a company that consisted of a fleet of fully equipped sea-going boats, many of which were manned by local sailors and ex-seamen. This became a seasonal business but employed the seamen all year round as the boats and equipment had to be maintained. In the early 1960s, the Industrial Development Authority gave financial aid to several new industries that established themselves in the Kinsale area.

FLUORESCENT

Fluorescent algae creating bioluminescence is perhaps the most talked about feature of Lough Hyne. Much of the glow is generated from a form of aquatic algae called dinoflagellates, which transform light energy from the sun into chemical energy. The lough is a well-sheltered body, warmed by sunlight, which means the algae can charge up in the day and glow at night. The best time to the experience the phenomenon is during the summer months.

Lough Hyne is Europe's first marine nature reserve and one of its few saltwater inland lakes. A narrow bottleneck, known as the Rapids, joins the lough to the sea at the end of Barloge Creek. The Rapids are very shallow and have an odd tide pattern. Water rushes in for four hours and flows out for eight and a half hours. It travels at speeds of 15km per hour.

Many marine biologists have studied the lough's wild diversity for over a century. In recent years, they have been joined by watersports enthusiasts from swimmers and sea kayakers to snorkellers and paddle boarders.

FOLLY

Leader's Folly is an impressive, ruinous aqueduct across the Dripsey River. Now hidden among the overgrowth with some pillars remaining, the general structure was erected in about 1860. Twelve piers supported a water chute intended to irrigate the land across the valley. The highest pier was 26m high. Some of the piers have been dismantled in the last century for building purposes. The water was piped for a distance of 3.2km cross-country. It was then fed into the chute and conveyed across the valley from Old Castle to Clonmoyle. It is said it did not operate very long. Mr Harry Leader, its developer, was a philanthropic type of individual and very often the object of his experiments was to provide employment for the poor people of the locality.

An amusing story is told of the erection of Leader's Folly. Masons were first employed for the building of the piers but their work was deemed unsatisfactory. Mr Leader then finished the project by direct labour. He employed several labourers and also accepted a number of boys who were on a juvenile rate of pay. One of the youths wore his father's hat and pants and was classed as a man. Soon all the boys were in their father's clothes and received the adult rate of pay without question. Mr Leader financed his schemes from a mortgage on his property. It was discovered after his death that he had no title to the land and the bank lost about £20,000.

FONT

In the archive of University College Cork lies the Elizabeth Friedländer Archival Collection. It contains the working papers of graphic designer Elizabeth Betty Friedländer (1903–84), famed for her intricate border designs and her custom-designed font 'Elizabeth'.

Berlin-born Friedländer began her venture into graphic design by studying art at the Berlin Academy. There she studied typography and calligraphy, under Emil Rudolf Weiss. She was then employed by the Jewish publishing house of Ullstein Verlag, Berlin, designing headings for its fashion journal, *Die Dame*.

In 1927–28 Elizabeth was asked to create a typeface for the Bauer Typefoundry, which was completed in 1938. Standard practice would have called the typeface after the designer's surname. However 'Friedländer' was deemed too Jewish for the time and it was instead announced as 'Elizabeth'.

In October 1936, with the introduction of Nazi regulations, Elizabeth moved to Milan and worked for the publisher Mondadori (1936–38) and for Editoriale Domus (from February 1937). She also designed book jackets and publicity materials.

In February 1939, Elizabeth arrived in London with a domestic service permit, which allowed her to work as a maid. With the assistance of Francis Meynell, she obtained employment at the advertising agency Mather & Crowther, later also doing 'black propaganda' for the Political Intelligence Department, Central Office of Information. Elizabeth also did freelance work for a number of publishers.

In June 1948, Elizabeth was assigned by Jan Tschichold, the new art director at Penguin Books, to carry out some title lettering and, most notably, to design patterned papers for covers of the Penguin Music Scores and Penguin Poets. During the next decade she drew roundels for the Penguin Classics series. From 1951 she was the calligrapher on the Royal Military College, Sandhurst, lettering rolls of honour. Her ornamental borders were produced by Linotype (1952) and Monotype ('The Friedländer borders', 1958).

In 1961, Friedländer moved to Kinsale (until her death), from where she continued to design bookplates, book jackets, catalogues and calligraphic maps, as well as lettering Irish proverbs on parchment. She died there in 1984.

FOOTPRINTS

Two adult footprints in the earth have fascinated locals in the Newmarket area in north Cork for decades. It was in the townland of Glenamuckla that the footprints appeared around 1920. They are connected to folklore concerning a murder during a very bitter family dispute about a small sum of money in the area thirty-two years before.

On 28 July 1888, James Rourke, farm labourer, was shot while he mowed hay. At the inquest that followed, farmer David McAuliffe related that he witnessed a man with a double-barrelled gun entering the field. There was an exchange of words, and James was shot. The man who fired the fatal shots is said to have emigrated swiftly to New York, where he worked under an assumed name, later entering the US Army and New York Fire Service.

In 1920, on the ditch where the murderer stood, footprints appeared in a supernatural fashion. Every means possible was used to clear the ditch of the markings, by both humans and animals. However, the grass grew again and they reappeared. Local priests were brought in and blessed the location but there was no success in eliminating the footprints. It was only in 2020 when the footprints finally disappeared.

FRAGMENT

Archaeologist Peter Woodman once remarked that much of the evidence for an early Mesolithic occupation of Munster has come from the Blackwater Valley in County Cork. His work details that they lived a hunter-gatherer lifestyle and utilised mainly flint to create stone tools. There is no sign that Mesolithic people created permanent structures.

Ireland's Site Monument Record documents that west of the town of Fermoy, at Castlehyde East, on the north side of the Blackwater River, a flint scatter was identified during a field study project. In addition, 18km west of Fermoy, in the townland of Kilcummer Lower, over 300 flint pieces were recovered during excavations by Liz Anderson. Most of these consisted of 'blades and blade fragments. Ten microliths were also found, which included rods and one scalene triangle, three microburins, two scrapers, a single-platformed core and much debitage.'

Between Kilcummer Lower and Fermoy, two more flint scatters were found along the Blackwater Valley, in the townlands of Conva and Castleblagh.

GAME

Scoubeen was an early form of modern hurling, which was practised in early historic Ireland. Over the succeeding centuries, different kinds of sticks were used to drive roughly made spheres over the most basic of roads or across grassland. The rules were simple. The quasi-ball had to be played to a predetermined spot in a parish. There were no limits to how many players played in a scoubeen match. Due to no stewards or officials overseeing the game, any arguments were settled by physical fights. Of course, first aid was in very short supply.

Scoubeen sticks were usually home-made, were of all outlines and sizes – and not everyone played with one. The home-made ball could be made of anything from wool woven around a centre of a cork to matted cow hair, to something similar to the present-day sliothar.

One could carry the ball in one's pocket, but such a play by a player would end up with his clothing being torn to bits. Having a team with fast runners was of great benefit as getting the ball to them and enabling them to pursue a solo run was significant. Players concentrating on their solo efforts had the prefix 'fuadach' connected to their surname.

In the 1870s, a legendary scoubeen match took place between north Cork players at Ballyhea and Charleville. Both sides chose local players and some even arrived from the heart of County Limerick. The match is said to have involved the vast number of 500 players and commenced at the hill of the Old Pike. The ball was thrown in and up went the cry, 'All for home'.

From the start, Ballyhea progressed well. Play continued until it was dragged into a meadow flooded to the depth of 30cm, across other landscape obstacles until it got as far the banks of the (Upper) Awbeg to a site named locally as Madigan's Marsh. It was here a serious fight broke out. No one was killed or seriously wounded but the Charleville side eventually conceded.

With the establishment of the Gaelic Athletic Association in 1884, the game of scoubeen rapidly disappeared.

GARDEN

On 10 June 1995, the impressive Liss Ard Sky Garden in the midst of a 50-acre estate area near Skibbereen fully opened to the general public. It took five years of planning, and the spending of an estimated £1.8 million. This unique space aimed to offer a whole new type of experience for tourists and locals alike and its many very special features are sure to enthral and interest. The estate was transformed from an area that was generally neglected during the previous fifty or more years and had in many places become overgrown with weeds and totally run down.

The directors of the Liss Ard Foundation, which has a wide membership, worked long and hard to develop the entire concept. They were principally Mr Veith Turske and his partner, Dr Claudia Meister, who is a qualified anthropologist, but, over the period, they have had considerable professional help from various experts and particularly the celebrated American artist James Turrell, who was described in the *Daily Telegraph* newspaper as the 'greatest artist of the 21st century'. The concept itself was developed by Turrell, who was responsible for all the architectural drawings involved.

The idea of the crater in the garden was modelled by Turrell on the only other existing such edifice in the world, the Roden Crater in the Arizona Desert, which Turrell himself has transformed and was described by one commentator as a 'Cathedral of the Skies'. To fully appreciate what is involved in the Sky Garden concept, one has to visit the crater and experience the vision of the sky that is offered from inside this vast construction.

The crater itself is beautifully finished and one enters by a long tunnel, at the end of which one ascends by steps made of Liscannor stone and eventually some white marble before arriving at the centre. Here there is a type of plinth, made of Kilkenny limestone, on which two people can lie down full length and view the sky from horizontal positions. Given the height of the crater walls, perhaps 30m, and the circular top edge, the viewer consequently can see nothing but the sky, a type of phenomenon not available under any other landscape arrangement and which confers a different aspect to the experience of light.

GENEROSITY

The scenic Kiskeam lies in north-west County Cork. A part of the area's folklore relates that during the Irish Great Famine, a generous woman could not bear to see starving, gaunt figures. While not telling her displeased husband, she fed those in need, but he found out eventually. His unhappiness led her to go on the run into the Cork countryside.

As the woman stumbled to the edge of a cliff face over the River Araglen, she hesitated about what to do next. Seeing her pursuer, she jumped and made it to the other side. Her pursuer was forced to stop his chase. Local folklore relates that the huge cliffs creaked and widened out to such an extent that the pursuer was forced to take the long way round. The name of the spot where the woman escaped has become known as Coiscéim na Caillí or 'the Footstep of the Old Woman', shortened to Kiskeam in time.

GIANT

In the heart of Cork Harbour is the place name Curraghbinny, which in Irish is Corra Binne, and which is reputedly named after the legendary giant called Binne. Legends tells that his cairn (called a '*Corra*' in Irish) is located in a burial chamber atop the now wooded hill. The cairn is not marked in the first edition Ordnance Survey map, but its existence was noted during the original survey in the Name Books compiled at that time. John Windle, the well-known Cork writer of the book *Historical and descriptive notices of the city of Cork and its vicinity: Gougaun-Barra, Glengariff and Killarney* (1839) and antiquarian of the early nineteenth century, mentions the site in his publications. There is no record, though, in his printed works or in his manuscripts preserved in the Royal Irish Academy Library, of any digging having taken place at the cairn.

In 1932, archaeologist Seán P. Ó'Riordáin and his team excavated the cairn. Except for a slight outer accumulation of soil, the cairn was composed of stone, most of which was local sandstone, there being only two pieces of limestone. As O'Riordáin's team worked into the cairn several large boulders lying on the ground came into view. It soon became apparent that the boulders formed part of a circle running concentric with the outer edge of the mound.

The most interesting discovery was made on the south side of the cairn. In a space between two stones of the kerb and a third lying just inside the team found, mixed with a thick layer of charcoal, some burnt bone fragments. Examination proved these to be human. The charcoal deposit with which the bones were found mixed did not extend under the neighbouring large stones. This showed that the fire was lit after the boulders had been placed in position. The cremated human bone found nearby was carbon dated roughly to be 4,000 years old.

Postcard of Kissing the Blarney Stone, Blarney Castle c.1900. (Cork Public Museum)

Blarney Castle. (Kieran McCarthy)

GIFT

Dripsey's Carrignamuck Castle was one of the strongholds erected by the Lords of Muskerry – chiefs of one of the three great stems into which the MacCarthy clan divided at a period before they erected stone castles. The first of the third stem was Dermod Mór MacCarthy, a son of Cormac MacCarthy Mór of the main line. Dermot was born in 1310 and in 1353 was acknowledged or created the 1st Lord of Muskerry by the English. The lands passed down to the 9th Lord of Muskerry, Cormac McTeige MacCarthy Láidir, who succeeded in 1449. He was a great builder and financed the construction of Blarney Castle, Carrignamuck and Kilcrea. It became the custom for the Lords of English lands to place some relative in each of their castles.

In the sixteenth century, Elizabeth I attempted to persuade Cormac MacCarthy to give up his lands, including Blarney, as proof of his loyalty to the Crown. Cormac repeatedly spoke wordy excuses, which the queen declared was Blarney talk.

Fast forward to Charles II, in 1658, he conferred the title of Earl of Clancarthy on the head of this family, the last of whom was dispossessed after the siege of Limerick. Hence the estate, comprising all Muskerry and its castles, was forfeited to the crown for the earl's adherence to the cause of James II. On the sale of the forfeited lands in 1692, the Hollow Sword Blade Company purchased all the land around this place, and more than 3,000 acres in the parish were allotted to a member of the company, and were held by his descendant, George Putland of Dublin. Blarney Castle was purchased in 1701 by Sir James Jefferies, Governor of Cork, who soon after erected a large and handsome house in front of it, which was the family residence for many years.

The story of the MacCarthys took a new course, especially as the late nineteenth century progressed and the rise of mass tourism to the castle began. The origins of the practice of kissing the Blarney Stone are obscure but seem to be rooted in antiquarian myth making in the nineteenth century.

H

HAG

Labbacallee, near Glanworth, translates as 'the hag's bed. Local folklore abounds with this ancient tomb of deeds of the old hag and those of her powerful husband, the mythic Druid, Mogh Ruith. One legend tells of a large boulder lying in the nearby river, which was deemed to be thrown by the hag at her fleeing husband, pinning him to the riverbed. When the tomb was excavated in 1934, it was found to contain the remains of a woman. Her skeleton was buried in the inner chamber of the tomb, while her head was found in the larger outer chamber.

Labbacallee is one of the biggest wedge-shaped gallery graves in the country. Such graves were erected in many parts of Ireland during the early Bronze Age around 1500 BC and are especially common in the south-west of Ireland. The tomb comprises of one large stone and one small chamber covered by three massive capstones. The burial chamber is surrounded by a stone cairn flanked by further upright stones in a U-formation. The tomb is aligned to the setting sun at the equinoxes, 22 March and 24 September, when day and night are of equal duration. On these days, given favourable weather conditions, the setting sun shines directly into the chamber and illuminates it with a beam of light.

During archaeological excavations in 1934, five burials were found – four unburned and one cremated. The principal one, that in the small chamber, was found undisturbed and consisted of an unburned skeleton of a woman placed at the bottom of the chamber and covered by loose stones and some earth. Near the right hand was the burned lower jaw of a pig. Other burned animal bones were of dogs. Fragments of earthenware vessels were found. Pieces of a thin well-baked pot, simply decorated with parallel lines, accompanied a young man's bones. Many pieces of a large and thicker vessel were found at the inner end of the large chamber and pieces of similar ware in the upper part of the smaller one. The excavation was aided by a government unemployment relief grant. The excavators were Messrs Liam Price and H.G. Leask.

Labbacallee wedge tomb, present day. (Kieran McCarthy)

* * *

An Chaileach Bhearra, translated as the Hag of Beara, is a prominent marker in the Beara Peninsula overlooking Coulagh Bay. She was deemed a goddess of sovereignty, who gave the kings the right to rule their lands.

According to the local information sign, she lived for seven periods of youth, one after another – so that every man who co-habited with her came to die of old age. Her grandsons and great grandsons were so many that they made up entire tribes and races – hence, her legend is woven into folklore across parts of Ireland and across the west coast of Scotland.

The advent of the arrival of Saint Caitiarin and Christianity was deemed a threat to her powers. Local folklore has it that one day after collecting sea wood along the shore of Whiddy Island, the Hag, on her return, encountered the priest asleep on a local hillock. She drew near to him and quietly took his prayer book and ran off. The saint caught up with her, re-acquired the prayer book and turned her into what is now a grey pillar stone – with her back to the hill and her face to the sea.

HAUNTED

In 1601, Cormac Tadhg McCarthy of Carrigaphooca Castle near Macroom was High Sheriff of Cork and had orders by his English overlords to search and capture all Irish rebels. Irish chieftain James Fitzgerald was targeted as a traitor. Cormac invited him to a feast in his castle pretending it was an effort to make peace.

During the feast, Fitzgerald was killed. In an effort to impress his English overlords, McCarthy ate the raw flesh of the chieftain, much to the horror of the guests who were in attendance. Defending his actions, McCarthy claimed that he had been possessed by an evil spirit that had come out of the rock upon which the castle was constructed.

On Cormac's death, it is said that his body began to haunt his former home, attacking anyone within the curtilage of the structure. The legend still lingers in the local area around the ruinous Carrigaphooca Castle.

Hag of Beara Rock, present day. (Kieran McCarthy)

HEADLESS

In the harbour of Leap there is a very small point known as Simon's Point. Simon was a land agent and he resided at Bán Léárian townland with his mother. At the appointed time, he collected the rents from the tenants and took the money to Cork city to the landlord. At that time, the nearest market for produce from the farm was in Cork and the only way of transport was by boat or horse.

There was a family of Donovans living in Myross. They were going on market day to the city and Simon arranged to travel with them. They all embarked at midnight on their journey. However, members of the Donovan family had decided to murder Simon and rob him early on the road, close to his home. They cut off his head and threw his head and body into the sea. When Simon did not return home, his mother raised an alarm.

After some time, Simon's headless body floated to the surface. It was picked up and the mother recognised it as Simon's. The Donovan family feared that the mother would offer the local constabulary information against them, so they watched her going to the well, approached her and drowned her. Then they buried her in a grave in the kitchen of her own home.

The Donovans were arrested and tried in Cork for the murder of Simon. There was scarcely any evidence against them, and there was no one who was present to recognise the body. In addition, the mother was reported missing.

The Donovans were freed and the constabulary were ordered from Cork to find the missing woman. When the Donovans got outside the city, one of the men offered to go back and confess to the murder of both Simon and his mother. He felt it better to have one hanged than the whole family. The women rejected the idea.

One of the women took off quickly, bound for Bán Léárian. She arrived there before the constabulary and got some friends to help her remove the body of Simon's mother from the grave underneath the kitchen. When the constabulary arrived they observed the empty grave. They searched around the grounds of the homestead but failed to find the body.

At that time, there were a number of men dredging sand in the harbour. According to the tide, they were often late coming up to Leap, and they were startled by a voice at Simon's point. They could see no one but they could plainly hear in Irish 'Cur mo Ceann, dteannta mo Coirp', or 'put my head along with my body'. They decided to drag the water close to where Simon's body had been found. They found the head and buried it in the same grave with Simon's body and the voice was never heard since.

HORSE

On the northern side of the bridge in Fermoy in north Cork is an elegant sculptural piece by bronze specialist artist Jarlath Daly, dedicated to John Anderson, who developed the town of Fermoy in the early nineteenth century. In 1791, John Anderson, having purchased two-thirds of the ancient manor, erected a hotel and houses, and laid the foundation of the town's future prosperity and growth.

The *Oxford Dictionary of National Biography* denotes that John Anderson (*c.*1747–1820) was born in western Scotland in poverty, the son of David Anderson, of Portland. He moved to Glasgow and after making £500 through dealing in herring in 1780 he moved to Cork city. Anderson quickly established himself as an export merchant in the provisions trade with a base on Lapp's Quay. Today Anderson's Quay is named in his honour. A £500 investment multiplied quickly and by 1789 he could successfully bid for, and set up, the first Irish mail coach service. This proved both reliable and profitable. The initial services were on routes from Dublin to Belfast and Dublin to Cork. The system was gradually extended countrywide. The first service from Dublin to Waterford took place in 1790.

John Anderson pioneered cheap passenger travel and had a monopoly on it. The mail coach was drawn by four horses and had seating for four passengers inside. Other passengers were later permitted to sit outside with the driver. The mail was kept in a box to the rear, where a Royal Mail post office guard stood. The mail coach was quicker than the stagecoach as it only stopped for delivery of mail and generally not for the comfort of the passengers. They were slowly phased out during the 1840s and '50s, their role being replaced by trains as the railway network expanded. Many of the mail coaches in Ireland were also eventually out-competed by Charles Bianconi's countrywide network of open carriages, before this system in turn succumbed to the railways.

✳ ✳ ✳

Established in the seventeenth century, Cahirmee Horse Fair in its heyday was one of the country's great horse fairs and attracted buyers from many parts of Europe, who were on the lookout for sturdy animals suitable for armies. Great scenes were seen on the roads on the fair morning. Crowds came from all over the district. Buyers came from all over Europe. Horses were brought from every quarter to be sold. Tradition has it that Napoleon Bonaparte's famous white charger, Marengo, was purchased by one of the military purchasing missions that regularly attended the event. Marengo was named after the Battle of Marengo in 1800.

S.A. Walker, in his book *Horses of Renown*, published in London in 1954, writes that the light grey or white Arab stallion called Marengo was imported from Egypt as a 6-year-old in 1799 after the Battle of Aboukir, and was descended from the famous El Naseri Stud. Another school of thought is that Marengo was bred in County Wexford. He was bred by Annesley Brownrigg of Annesley Park and was foaled in 1796. There is a claim that the 16 hands high Marengo was sold to a French officer before 1900 for 100 guineas and that a bunch of hairs from the horse's tail was preserved by the Brownrigg family who bred him. Both the latter claims are not proof positive, but buyers did come from Wexford to buy horses.

Napoleon is reputed to have ridden Marengo early in the Battle of Waterloo but the animal received a hip wound and was replaced on the battlefield. Marengo was captured after Napoleon fled. The horse was eventually brought back to England, where he was bought by General Angerstein of the Grenadier Guards, who put him to stud. The horse died in 1831 and today his skeleton is on display at the National Army Museum in London.

Cahirmee Fair is still an annual occasion, being held on 12 July (now a one-day event), when the streets of Buttevant are filled with people and horses.

* * *

In 1752, the name steeplechase originated in a horse race first held between two steeples, that of St John's Church in Buttevant to that of Saint Mary's Church in the town of Doneraile. The two church steeples were among the tallest buildings in the area.

Cornelius O'Callaghan and Edmund Blake were at dinner at Buttevant Castle, enjoying the company. They made a bet between themselves to race from one steeple to another. The landscape comprised fields, streams and river, and the distance was approximately 6.5km. The prize was more than 600 gallons of port. It is not recorded who was the first to touch the base of the steeple in Doneraile.

However, the race inspired a new sport, with steeplechase races becoming a tradition. By the early nineteenth century, races over fences on prepared race tracks were being organised in England. In March 1830, the first recognised English National Steeplechase took place. Such steeplechase races can also be known as point-to-point races.

* * *

Leap in Irish is Léim Uí Dhonnabhain, or O'Donovan's Leap. In recent decades, the full name has been reduced to An Léim or Léim (Leap). At the western side of the village is located a deep gorge over which, according to myth, an O'Donovan leaped on horseback while being pursued by British soldiers. The gorge divides West from East Carbery, and a local saying notes 'beyond the Leap, beyond the Law'.

HULK

It was in the Great Famine period of 1847 that Spike Island in Cork Harbour first became a convict establishment. For many years before prisoners were transported to Botany Bay and other penal settlements, many were shipped from Cork Harbour, where a 'convict hulk' or prison ship was established as a temporary place of detention while prisoners awaited shipment abroad. The convict hulk was named HMS *Surprise*. *Surprise* was a decommissioned British naval frigate. It was brought into service in May 1823 and could take in 500 men.

During this time, all convict ships sailed from Cork. Prisoners imprisoned in Dublin gaols would be shipped by brig to Cork. In April 1825, a new hulk called *Essex* was authorised in Dublin Harbour. From then on, all prisoners from the northern and eastern counties of the country were imprisoned on *Essex*. *Surprise* was used to detain prisoners from the western and southern counties.

Convict ships were to depart from Kingstown (now Dún Laoghaire) in Dublin Harbour and from Cove, now Cobh, in Cork Harbour. Some ships took on prisoners from both hulks. They would gather prisoners from *Essex* in Kingstown and then sail to Cove to collect additional prisoners if the convict ship had not been able to meet its quota.

Circumstances on both hulks were very harsh. Rations were inadequate, with a number of reports describing starvation and the poor health of prisoners. Clothing was entirely insufficient and prisoners, in many cases, scarcely wore anything. The clothing was governed by the prison administration and produced by male and female prisoners at the Cork Convict Depot. The fabric utilised was fustian, a cloth consisting of cotton and flax and not appropriate to withstand the cold. Many convicts landed in New South Wales with their clothes in tatters.

IDEAS

To the east of Cork Harbour lies the historic village of Cloyne. On the margins of the village lies St Colman's Church. In 1734, one of its most famous clerics and bishops took up office there – philosopher George Berkley (1685–1753).

Born in Kilkenny, at the age of 15, he became a student at Trinity College, Dublin. At the age of 22, he was made a fellow of the college and was ordained shortly afterwards in the Anglican Church. As revealed in his surviving notebooks (found in the manuscripts collection at the British Library, London), George developed a deep interest in philosophy and wrote critical responses to the leading philosophers of his day, such as René Descartes, Thomas Hobbes, John Locke, Nicolas Malebranche, Isaac Newton and others. In 1709, George published his first important work, *An Essay Towards a New Theory of Vision*. It was an important work examining the psychology of vision.

In his mid-twenties, George published his most well known and enduring works, the *Treatise concerning the Principles of Human Knowledge* (1710) and the *Three Dialogues between Hylas and Philonous* (1713).

In 1720, in the midst of pursuing a four-year tour of Europe as tutor to a young man, Berkeley wrote *De Motu*, a pamphlet on the philosophical foundations of mechanics. After his continental tour, George came back to Ireland and took up his position at Trinity until 1724, when he was appointed Dean of Derry.

At this time, Berkeley commenced his project for founding a college in Bermuda. In 1728, he set sail for America with his new bride, Anne Forster. Unfortunately, the political support for George's project dissipated and in 1731 they returned to Britain. While in America, though, George wrote *Alciphron*, a work directed against the 'free-thinkers' whom he believed to be threats to established Anglicanism.

Shortly after returning to London, George penned the *Theory of Vision, Vindicated and Explained* and *The Analyst*, the latter of which was a critique of the foundations of Newton's calculus.

In 1734 when he was made Bishop of Cloyne, George wrote his last work. Entitled *Siris* (1744), it had a threefold aim – first, to establish the virtues of tar-water as a medical panacea, and second, to provide scientific background supporting the effectiveness of tar-water, and to inspire the reader toward contemplation of God.

George died in 1753. He had just moved to Oxford to oversee his son George and his education. His son was the only one of his three children who survived childhood.

IDENTITY

In the village of Rockchapel in the very north-west of the county lies the lively cultural heritage centre, Bruach na Carraige. Its work promotes the traditions and culture of what is called the Sliabh Luachra region. Through the organisation's website, one can view a mapped out and rich cultural trail to embark on.

The borders of north-west Cork, east Kerry and along the south-western edges of County Limerick are known as Sliabh Luachra and are set on geographical uplands. It is recorded that the kingdom of Luachra was initially written about in the *Annals of Inisfallen* in AD 534, when the King of Luacar beat Tuathal Moel nGarb, and again in AD 741, with the death of Cuaine, Abbot of Ferna, and Flan Feórna, son of Cormac, King of Luachra.

By the Middle Ages, Sliabh Luachra was only known for its impoverished agricultural land, which was compounded by high rainfall, its high-altitude location, and a myriad of bogs and heathlands.

In the late sixteenth and early seventeenth centuries, as dispossession of lands continued apace with the English Munster Plantation, there was an influx into the marginalised uplands. Over a space of a few years, a distinctive culture emerged in story-telling, poetry, traditional music and dance.

For centuries there were no roads leading into the area. It was notable for hiding early nineteenth-century Irish rebels and outlaws. Such a situation encouraged the local British authorities to construct new lines of road and indeed build villages such as Kingwilliamstown (renamed Ballydesmond in 1951).

Edward Walsh (1805–50) was the most prolific publicist of his generation on the poetry, legends and general Gaelic culture of the Cork–Kerry border areas. The area to which he belonged, by birth, and from which, he was never detached in spirit, was Sliabh Luachra. Its musicians, song-makers, singers, and dancers delighted him in his youth. He immortalised much of their talented creations.

An tAthair Padraig Ó Dúinnín, compiler of Dinneen's *Irish-English Dictionary*, was born in Corrin, Shrone. This dictionary today persists as a key publication in keeping the Irish language a living one. Writer and Professor Daniel Corkery, author of *The Hidden Ireland*, wrote that Sliabh Luachra was the literary capital of Ireland.

ILLEGAL

Old folklore tells of *Poitín*, an illegal spirit, being produced discreetly in the nineteenth century in the heart of the Gearagh near Macroom. The reason for it's illegality dates back to 1660, when a tax was placed on spirits that were distilled. To avoid the tax, there was a movement to make *poitín* in homesteads and hidden away areas such as forests and valleys.

Further suppression of poitín making in the middle of the eighteenth century kept this illegal spirit-making alive, especially as further taxes were introduced on the legal side of *poitín* production. In particular, the sale of *poitín*, legally and illegally, could add to small farms' incomes and support the paying of rent.

Poitín was a mix of ingredients, consisting of potato, malt yeast, barley, sugar and water. This mix was then fermented together in a wooden barrel for three weeks. After the distillation process, the resulting drink was a clear alcoholic spirit.

The years of Ireland's Great Famine and 'Black 1847' brought about a decrease in the growth of potatoes, and as a result a decline in the making of *poitín* took place in the decades to follow. Despite this, it continued to be made in the Gearagh illegally well into the 1960s.

INFATUATION

Sarah Siddons Tower, built on the coastal edge of Rostellan Estate overlooking Cork Harbour, is a place dedicated to the memory of the famous English actress. Sarah was well known on English and Irish stages, being a travelling thespian with fellow actors from provincial theatre to provincial theatre. She gained a reputation for being the Queen of Tragedy. She played in Cork three times for the enormous sum of 40 guineas a go. The Earl of Inchiquin, owner of Rostellan Estate, greatly admired her and built a tower in her honour on the grounds of Rostellan Castle. She, in turn, was apparently entranced by Rostellan and its scenery.

INFLATION

Known as 'the Fearless Frogman', Irish-born Paul Boyton pursued daredevil acts in open water while 'encased' in a vulcanised rubber suit. The wearer inflated it by blowing into air tubes. This suit permitted him to float on the water and then he could move forward while using an oar.

Paul was confident that the apparatus could protect hundreds of lives if more of the public were aware of it. To attract media attention, Paul decided to carry out a number of high-profile stunts.

In the port of New York in October 1874, Paul's stunt was rejected by several ships' captains. They did want to allow a man to jump off a ship into the Atlantic Ocean for fear he would drown. To avert any further refusal, he boarded a ship

St Olan's Cap, present day. (Kieran McCarthy)

called the *Queen* as a stowaway. He hid in an unoccupied bunk until the following day after departure.

Arriving on deck, Paul quickly put on his apparatus, which comprised a waterproof rubber bag filled with ten days' provisions, and a double-headed axe attached to his waist in order to oppose any shark attacks. Paul did not even get as far as the ship's railings when he was discovered and detained in the crew quarters by Captain Bragg.

During the voyage, Paul persuaded the captain to let him try out the apparatus just off the Irish coast. So, on the evening of 21 October, Paul jumped into the ocean off Cork's Sherkin Island. A strong gale blew Paul towards the shore.

After two hours at sea, the storm blew him into the cliffs near Baltimore. Paul climbed onto the land and made his way towards the lights of the village. His arrival in his rubber suit shocked those he encountered, especially the local coastguard, who thought Paul had concussion after being shipwrecked.

Paul's efforts to get media attention worked. His story was picked up by the *New York Herald,* and soon after, international fame found him. The following year, in 1875, Paul, in his inflatable rubber suit, took on the English Channel and in 1878, the Straits of Gibraltar. In 1881, he took on a 3,580-mile stretch of the Mississippi River.

INSCRIBED

The Ballycrovane Ogham stone is 5.3m tall and towers above the local landscape of the Beara Peninsula. Weathered by wind and rain erosion, on the eastern facing section of the stone there is an ogham inscription which reads: *MAQI DECCEDDAS AVI TURANIAS*, which translates to 'Of the son of Deich a descendant of Torainn'. The Ogham writing itself may have been added in early Christian times, whilst the main stone was possibly erected in the Bronze Age. The stone is so tall that it goes well into the ground beneath in order to keep it upright.

✳ ✳ ✳

Just north of the present village of Aghabullogue in mid-County Cork is the townland of Coolineagh, or Cúilín Aoidh or 'Hugh's Recess'. Bisected by a roadway, in that area was an important early medieval ecclesiastical site in the catchment area of the Lee. It was associated with St Eolang (Olan), who according to hagiographical tradition (the study of saints), was St Finbarr's teacher. The site is noted in the various biographies of St Finbarr.

The surviving remains of the ecclesiastical site comprises a relatively modern church within a rectangular graveyard. A segment of the original circular enclosure can be traced in the south-western quadrant of the site. Today, the fragmentary remains of two successive Church of Ireland parish churches of Aghabullogue survive in the graveyard. Only the sod-covered remains of the earlier St Olan's Church survive, which was initially built about 1690.

In the graveyard is St Olan's Cap, an upright stone measuring 1.5m high with Ogham inscription. A second stone was placed on top of it (now cemented in place) and was the subject of interesting fertility rituals. It was alleged to be an unfailing object to have in your house in childbirth situations and was also used for female illnesses. The associated rituals were occasionally the cause of official clerical disapproval, leading to its removal at one stage in the nineteenth century. Today, the stone can be seen to have been much rubbed by human hands.

JACK

Of the more interesting characters who served time in Cork Harbour's Spike Island prison in the mid-nineteenth century was James Gray, a 28-year-old thief from Manchester. He was nicknamed Jack-in-the-Box. Gray assembled a big wooden box with hinges and springs that allowed him to open it from the inside. He would address the box to a person in Cork, Belfast or Limerick. He always took care to pen on the box 'this side up – with care'. He would conceal himself inside the box while a collaborator took it to a railway station or packing office.

Once the box was safely stored in the luggage compartment of a train, or in the hold of a ship, Gray opened and climbed out of the box in order to go through the surrounding luggage and pilfer any expensive materials that he could fit inside his box. When he had completed his task, he clambered back inside the box and resumed his journey.

Gray's thefts were unnoticed until one of his lodgers read about a reward in the newspaper for the retrieval of some expensive shawls that the lodger had seen in Gray's house. The lodger went to the police and reported Gray. During an examination of the dwelling they discovered the box. In 1856, Gray was sent to Spike Island prison for four years' penal servitude.

JAPANESE

John William Fenton (1828–90) was born in Kinsale. His career led him to be bandmaster of Britain's 1st Battalion, 10th Regiment of Foot. He went to Japan as a bandmaster with the British Army in 1868, the year of the Meiji Restoration. In the following year, he started training the brass band in Japan for soldiers of the Satsuma clan at Myoko-ji Temple in Yokohama. The band became the country's first military band.

When Emperor Meiji inspected the troops, consisting of four clans including Satsuma, the military band played for the first time in public. On that occasion,

John composed a ceremonial melody to accompany the poem 'Kimigayo'. Over time, the melody became accepted as the national anthem, although the current anthem is different from John's original version. John is also known as the father of brass band music in Japan and is celebrated for his musical contribution to the country.

JUSTICE

Nora Herlihy (1910–88) was a primary school teacher originally from the Duhallow area in north-west County Cork. She taught in schools in the poorest parts of Dublin. With an interest in social justice, she travelled to America, where she studied the Credit Union movement. At the time, it was said that Credit Unions had played a big part in the United States in protecting wage earners from loan sharks. Credit Unions were co-operative savings banks but provided loans at reasonable and clearly understood rates of interest. In November 1954, Nora wrote to the Credit Union National Association (CUNA) in America mentioning that the society she represented was interested in the possibility of adopting the idea of Credit Unions in Ireland.

Nora initiated talks about Credit Unions with the National Co-Operative Council in Ireland. The National Council decided to set up a sub-committee to examine the whole field of Credit Unions and their application to Irish life. Nora was secretary of this sub-committee and at the third meeting she proposed that they call themselves the Credit Union Extension Service. That became the spearhead of the Credit Union movement in Ireland. In 1958, the first Credit Union was established on Donore Street, Dublin, under Nora's guiding influence. From small beginnings, Credit Unions in Ireland now have a membership of 3 million and total assets of €14 billion. There are currently 9,500 voluntary officers and 3,500 permanent employees of Irish Credit Unions.

KINDRED

For decades there was only one solitary public monument in Midleton – the monument dedicated to the losses at Clonmult during the Irish War of Independence in 1921. It is located at the northern end of Main Street. In 1998, a second monument was added, just a couple of metres from the Clonmult Monument. Then, in the early 2000s came the Gyrator, on the site of the former Goose's Acre, again, not far from the Clonmult Monument. From 2014 to 2015 Midleton installed five sculptures or monuments, four of them in the area around the Clonmult Monument and one isolated in the park on the Bailick Road.

In their 2013 budget, Midleton Town Council approved a number of capital projects for the period 2013–15. New sculptures were commissioned, with the help of an open competition for entries, to help the promotion of history, heritage and tourism in the town. Both 'Geese Attacking Young Boy' and the sculpted piece of 'Nellie Cashman' are located at the Goose's Acre. The 'Fenian Man' is to represent the Irish 1798 Rebellion by the United Irishmen movement. The 'Fair Green' is a concrete pillar, finished with a granite face 3m high and has five oversized sheep situated around it.

The fifth sculpture represents a US Choctaw Nation gift of aid to Ireland during the Irish Great Famine. It is a bowl structure made of eagle wings, 5 to 6m in height, entitled 'Kindred Spirits' and created by artist Alex Pentak. The Choctaw Nation raised $170, which is comparable to thousands of dollars today. The money was sent to Ireland towards food for the starving Irish. This was enormous generosity on their behalf as, sixteen years before, the Choctaw people were forced by US President Andrew Jackson to leave their ancestral lands and march over 800km. Many did not make the journey and died.

In June 2017, the sculpture was officially unveiled and dedicated by Chief Gary Batton, of the Choctaw Nation, Assistant Chief Jack Austin Junior and Councillor Seamus McGrath, County Mayor of Cork. They were supplemented by a twenty-strong delegation from the Choctaw Nation.

'Kindred Spirits' by Alex Pentak, present day. (Kieran McCarthy)

KING

Just over 24km to the south-west of Macroom lies Currane Hill, which is deemed to be the burial site of Lugaid MacCon. He was one of two ancient High Kings from the province of Munster. The cairn was known as Carn MacCon. In 1950, all of the stones were used to build a cross in commemoration of the Marian Year and the erection of a large mast also damaged the historic nature of the site.

Lugaid MacCon was an ancestor of the Erainn, a set of ancient families of Celtic rulers of Ireland. Reputedly he was born in what is now the Enniskeane area of west Cork. He reigned as High King from AD 195 to 225, for the most part in the east, south-east and south-west of Ireland. He ruled as High King of Tara for thirty years. Across a vast amount of land, political rivalries were commonplace.

Lugaid was expelled from Tara by his successor, Cormac mac Airt, whose father Lugaid had killed years earlier in battle. Lugaid returned to west Cork. He was murdered at a place called the Red Fort in the townland known as Derriga. The name Derriga derives from the Irish *Dearg Rath*, which translates as Red Fort. The townland is close to Ballineen.

Lugaid was cremated, and his ashes were buried on the 228m-high Currane Hill. In the mid-nineteenth century, the tomb was broken into and his urn was discarded. In recent years, the active Ballineen and Enniskeane Heritage Group has re-identified where Lugaidh's cairn once stood, and this has been supported by local farmers in the local area.

When Cormac succeeded Lugaid as High King, he then turned to creating a new alliance with elderly chieftain Fionna MacCumhail. He offered his daughter, Gráinne's hand in marriage. However, Gráinne was more in love with Fionn's young lieutenant, Diarmuid Uí Duibhne. Gráinne and Diarmuid eloped.

After absconding from Fionn, Gráinne and Diarmuid returned to County Cork, settling for a time in a cave halfway up what is now present-day Owen Hill, several kilometres from Enniskeane and 8km west of Dunmanway. Eventually, the act of the elopement caught up with Diarmuid; he was hunted down and killed. It is said that he is buried under a tumulus near Murragh Graveyard, which is just 4.8km to the north-east of Currane Hill.

KITCHEN

On the road from Canovee to Coachford, along the south bank of the River Lee, the explorer comes to a crossroads where a plaque denotes the site of Soup House Cross Roads. The memorial in Canovee was erected by the local historical society in 1997 to mark the giving out of soup in the area during the Great Famine. In that year, the 150th anniversary of the Great Famine was commemorated with new museums and memorials appearing across the Irish landscape and across the world.

In her work on the Great Famine in Cork's barony area of Muskerry, titled *Famine in Muskerry, an drochshaol: an outline of conditions in the sixteen parishes of Macroom Poor Law Union, Co. Cork, during the Great Famine, 1845-'51* (1997), Máire MacSuibne notes that the population of County Cork declined from 854,118 to 649,903 – almost 24 per cent – through death and emigration. Cork city's population increased from 80,720 to 85,745 as a result of the influx of rural migrants.

Eleven Poor Law Unions were established in County Cork under the 1838 Poor Law Act. Six more unions were added in 1850. A union covered approximately 42km in area throughout the country. The unions were run by a Board of Guardians – resident magistrates, elected representatives and medical officers.

Canovee was in the Macroom Poor Law Union. Unfortunately, the Macroom Union was poorly organised because neighbouring Kilmichael belonged to

Dunmanway Union, while parishes like Donoughmore and Matehy, more than 32km distant, were attached to Macroom.

One of the central relief stations within the union was the workhouse at Macroom. The cost of running it was levied on ratepayers, hence expenses were kept to a minimum. William H.W. Hedges of Macroom Castle was the chairman of the Macroom Workhouse.

Workhouse residents were given branded clothes bearing the name 'Macroom Union' across the back. They were also required to wear special Glengarry caps. All male paupers had their hair shorn, supposedly in the interest of cleanliness. Workhouse paupers were employed in breaking stones, knitting, making fishing nets, uniforms and bags, or growing vegetables in the Union grounds while the children received education.

A reporter from the *Cork Examiner* visited Macroom on 20 December 1847 and told of the 'sufferings and privations of the appalled and afflicted resident'. Many inmates suffered from severe dysentery 'superinduced by the too frequent use of unboiled cabbage and other vegetables'. The children were crying for food. To conserve some warmth in the bitter winter weather, families huddled together on heaps of hay, straw or rushes, with no covering but their wretched clothes.

By 1848 Macroom Union struggled to remain functional. The burial ground at the workhouse was overfull despite the use of quicklime to hasten decomposition. Local cemeteries found it difficult to deal with the huge numbers of burials. In post-famine times, the 1851 census identified 407 unemployed persons classified as having no specified occupation and living outside of the workhouse. Some were occupied locally as agricultural labourers or building labourers. A total of 641 could not read or write. Indeed, these were dark days for the people of Macroom.

LAMENT

Adjacent to the ruinous church tower of Kilcrea Abbey, near Ovens, is the gravestone of the famous Arthur O'Leary's tomb. It bears the following inscription: 'Lo Arthur Leary, Generous, Handsome, Brave, slain in His Bloom lies in this humble grave. Died May 4th 1773 aged 26 years.'

The local interpretative panel reveals that Arthur was born at Raleigh, near Macroom, in 1747. He was a member of a prosperous family who, despite the penal laws, managed to retain extensive land holdings between Macroom and Gougane Barra. Denied educational and career opportunities at home because of the penal laws, Arthur, like many Catholic young men of good family, went abroad, where he served as a captain in the Hungarian Hussars.

In 1767 on his return from service abroad, Arthur married Eiblín Dubh Ní Chonaill, aunt of 'the Liberator' Daniel O'Connell. Arthur was killed in 1773 at Carriganima near Macroom by soldiers accompanying a local magistrate, Abraham Morris (also known as Morrison) of Hanover Hall, allegedly for refusing to sell his horse to Morris for £5, a legal technicality designed to prevent Roman Catholics owning horses fit for military service. In fact, his death was the culmination of a bitter and personal feud between the two men, caused by Art's assertive behaviour and Morris's determination to keep the penal laws alive. Morris had to stand trial for murder but was acquitted.

A celebrated lament in Irish, attributed to Arthur's wife Eiblín Dubh, '*Caoineadh Airt Uí Laoghaire*', is an emotionally powerful description of her reaction to his death. The tragic appeal of the poem has earned it a lasting place in Irish literature and ensured that Arthur will not be forgotten. '*Caoineadh Airt Uí Laoghaire*', or 'The Lament for Art Ó Laoghaire', is an Irish keen, or dirge. It has been described as one of the greatest poems written in either Ireland or Britain during the eighteenth century.

LANDMARK

For centuries, the famous landmark of the Old Head of Kinsale has been known to travellers. According to the Chronicles of Eri, Cearmna, brother of Sobairce, reigned in a rock-bound stronghold as King of Southern Ireland from 893 to 854 BC. The headland became known as Dún Cearmna, or Cearnma's Fort.

Cearmna was slain by Eochaidh Faobhar Glas (Eochaidh the blue-speared) in battle at the fort. Cearmna's foster son Connall held Dún Cearmna with other forts in Munster. It was held down to the close of the thirteenth century by the Hiberno Norse. They called it Oldernasse, meaning Old Head-ness, being the Scandinavian for a headland or promontory. The word 'ness' also occurs frequently in Scottish topography.

The Anglo-Norman family De Courcey, whom the surrounding barony was called after, changed their surnamed to MacPatrick and the Old Head fortress became Dún Mhic Phadraig, or MacPatrick's Fort.

In old Spanish, Portuguese, Italian and Dutch maps, the head is marked and called 'the Old Head' in their languages. In a Spanish document, it is described

Old Head of Kinsale Lighthouse, present day. (Kieran McCarthy)

as Cabo de Velbo, translated as the Cape of Light, derived from the beacon that burned on its summit from time immemorial.

In 1658, a recommendation was made by the Lord Deputy of Ireland for a lighthouse on the Head of Kinsale as the neighbouring bays were found to be very hazardous. The recommendation was not considered and it was only in 1665 that Robert Reading was empowered to erect lighthouses at or near Dublin, Carrigfergus, Waterford and Kinsale, and to maintain them during the night for the protection of shipping. Reading erected four lighthouses in all.

The current lighthouse was erected in 1853. In 1989, businessman John O'Connor purchased the entire headland of 220 acres for the princely sum of just €300,000. A scenic golf course was built upon the headland in 1993 and opened for play in 1997.

LEGENDARY

In the rural settlement landscape of early medieval Ireland (AD 400–1100), ringforts were a significant feature. Perhaps only a third of these settlements survive in their overgrown and remaining earthen banks. One site in the Bandon region has teased archaeologists for decades, that of Garranes.

Through legend, history and archaeology, Garranes is deemed a royal site. Historians have pieced together that the central ringfort was Rath Raithleann, the seat of the small kingdom of Uí Echach Mumhan. Such a kingdom is remembered in bardic poetry from the later medieval period. One such poem tells of its foundation by the fifth-century King of Munster named Corc. There is also the link to Cian, who was a son-in-law of Brian Ború, the famed Irish leader at the Battle of Clontarf in 1014.

In 1938, Professor Brendan O'Riordáin of University College Cork conducted an archaeological excavation of a large trivallate ringfort. Its finds presented indications that the settlement site was one of high status during the fifth and sixth centuries. Pottery and glass vessels imported from Atlantic France and the Mediterranean world were uncovered. The dig also uncovered that there were workshops on the site for the production of bronze ornaments, with enamel and glass working as well as signs of farming.

Such connection with the late Roman world helps in the understanding of how Christianity and literacy in southern Ireland spread.

Between 2011 and 2018, an interdisciplinary project took place in the Garranes area, whereby more archaeological surveys and excavation were carried out. These were buoyed by several specialist studies. The project was written up and edited by Professor William O'Brien and Nick Hogan.

LINES

What is left in Kilcolman near Doneraile in north Cork is an eerily ruined tower house wrapped in ivy. It was the former home of Elizabethan writer Edmund Spenser. He was born in London in 1552. Twenty-eight years later, he landed in Ireland to serve as secretary to Lord Deputy Grey, at that time in the midst of defeating the power of the Fitzgeralds of Desmond. Following the plantation of Munster, he was allocated a 3,000-acre estate at Kilcolman near Fermoy.

Edmund excelled in the pastoral and allegorical media. Even today, he is still considered one of the major poets of the Elizabethan literary renaissance. His prominent poems are *The Shepeardes Calendar*, 1579, and *The Fairie Queene*, which was half-finished at roughly six books, the first three appearing in 1590, the remainder in 1596. *The Fairie Queene* was devoted to Queen Elizabeth.

His best-known prose tract was composed in 1596 and published posthumously in 1633. It was called *A View of the Present State of Ireland*.

Kilcolman Castle remained the Spenser family seat until 1598, when it had to be summarily abandoned to the invading army of Owney MacRory O'Moore, sent from the north by Hugh O'Neill. Spenser returned to London in a dejected state. A month later, in January 1599, he was dead.

LOVERS

Sarah Curran was the daughter of John Philpott Curran, a parliamentary orator, who was born in Newmarket in 1750 and lived at Priory, almost 2km from the town. Sarah first encountered Irish patriot Robert Emmet in 1801, and her romantic affair with him endured until his execution two years later. Much of it was done at a distance, for Emmet was out of the country for a substantial time and when at home he was busy with his plans for a rebellion against English rule.

Inheriting stock to the value of £1,500 from his father, Dr Emmet, Robert transformed it into cash, and in a house in Dublin he had pikes, rockets and hand grenades produced en masse. One of his first ventures was to undertake an attack, exploding a portion of a house, killing one man and injuring others.

Robert resided full-time on the premises. On 23 July 1803, the day appointed for the rising, not more than 100 insurgents assembled with an uncontrolled mob. They mounted an attack on Dublin Castle. They shot dead a Colonel Brown and rushed upon a carriage containing Lord Kilwarden, the Lord Chief Justice of Ireland, his daughter and the Rev. Mr Wolfe. Lord Kilwarden and Mr Wolfe were murdered.

On hearing of the outrage, Emmet rushed from the head of his party and brought the lady to a nearby house for safety. The leaders lost control of the mob and Robert and his companions left them and fled to the County Wicklow hills.

Robert Emmet was subsequently arrested. He had two of Sarah's letters on him when captured and these proved most incriminating to himself and involved the Curran family. While in prison, he tried to induce his jailer to deliver a letter to Sarah, but the official gave it to the Attorney General instead.

Statue of Sarah Curran, present day. (Kieran McCarthy)

On hearing of this Emmet, offered to plead guilty and speak no word of defence if the authorities would permit his letter to reach its destination. The offer was rejected, and he was taken to trial for high treason and sentenced to be executed. He will forever be remembered in Irish history for his passionate speech from the dock.

After his execution, Sarah was thrown out of her home by her family and came to Cork to live with the Penrose family in Tivoli. It was during this time that she met Captain Henry Sturgeon. Without means of her own, and disowned by her family, she had little option but to consider marriage as a way out of an unfortunate situation. She accepted his proposal.

The marriage took place in Glanmire Parish Church and the newly married couple then left for England. Captain Sturgeon was later posted to Sicily. Sarah became pregnant while in Sicily and the baby was born aboard ship during Sarah's trip home because of failing health. The child died on landing at Portsmouth in January 1808.

Sarah only outlived the baby by four months. She died in Hythe in Kent on 5 May 1808, aged only 26. The cause of death is believed to be consumption. Her remains were brought back to her native Newmarket for burial in the old Protestant churchyard. A headstone marks the spot, while a statue in her memory can be viewed at the entrance to Newmarket town.

LURED

At one side of Dunworley Bay in the eastern part of Clonakilty Bay there dwelt an infamous 'wrecker', who in order to lure vessels to their doom would on stormy nights tie a lantern to the horn of a cow. The cow, having one leg strapped up and being led round in a circle, presented the appearance on a dark night of the light of a ship at sea. The man often succeeded in his deed and on one occasion, he lured inside the bay a vessel having on board a valuable cargo of gold dust and ivory.

Tradition has it that a boy survived the wreck and lived long enough to relate to a native, who showed him kindness, what had happened. He told his rescuer that the captain, as soon as he realised that he was trapped and that his ship was going to pieces, ordered the gold dust, which was in strong chests, to be lashed with chains to heavy pieces of cannon and sunk. He is also reputed to have pointed out the spot where treasure had been stored on the coast and this was linked later with the actual finding of gold cups.

M

MANUSCRIPT

On 25 June 1642, Louis Boyle, second son of Richard Boyle, Earl of Cork, wrote to his father from Bandon giving a description of the seizing of the castles of Kilbrittain and Coolmain by the troops under his command. He signed the letter with a postscript of a single line: 'I present your Lordship with a manuscript found at Kilbritten.'

The book Louis found, was written and compiled for Finghin MacCarthy Riabhach about 1480 and was preserved in the archives of Kilbrittain Castle, which was the chief seat of MacCarthy Riabhach. The *Book of Lismore* is notable for a series of saints' lives and the text of *Agallamh na Senórach*, whose title has been translated in English as *Tales of the Elders of Ireland* or *The Dialogue of the Ancients of Ireland*.

In June 1629, Michael Ó Cleirigh, Chief of the Four Masters, was in Timoleague Friary copying the lives of saints from the book, which had been borrowed for him from Kilbrittain Castle. Ó Cleirigh, in his haste to preserve the records of Ireland, stayed but a few days in Timoleague. A few months later, the friars had to flee from Timoleague. Religious persecution was again in full swing. No doubt the book had been returned to Kilbrittain before then, and was kept safe there until Louis Boyle decided to send it to his father.

Richard Boyle, Earl of Cork, probably gazed at his new acquisition. However, from 1642 until 1814, the book disappeared off the public radar. Then, in that year, it was found lying with a crozier in a wooden box in a walled-up passage in Lismore Castle by workmen engaged in repairing the building.

When discovered in 1814, the book had been damaged by damp and mice, and it was thought that some portions of it disappeared at that time. In 1815, the then agent to the Duke of Devonshire, Colonel Currey, lent the book to poet Donnacha Ó Floinn of Shandon Street in Cork. O'Floinn worked on it, gave it the name *Book of Lismore* and returned it to Lismore in the following year, but it seems that some portions of it disappeared while it was in his custody.

The missing portions were acquired by Thomas Hewitt of Cork city's Summerhill House. Sometime after 1853, John Windele read a paper on these portions to the Cork Cuverian Society in January 1855, in which he surmised that they were part of a different manuscript from the *Book of Lismore*. The Cork fragment, as it came to be known, was restored in 1860 and incorporated with the main body of the book in Lismore.

The Cavendish family and their ancestors kept the book at Lismore Castle, County Waterford, and in more recent times at Chatsworth House in Derbyshire.

The manuscript's owners have previously lent it for scholarly use since the nineteenth century, not only to Cork's scribal circle, but to institutions such as the Royal Irish Academy, the British Museum and to University College Cork, where it was placed on public exhibition for the first time in 2011. In 2020, the book was donated by the Trustees of the Chatsworth Settlement to University College Cork, where the original and a digital copy can be viewed.

MARRIAGE

Cape Clear Island is full of historic structures and ancient monuments. However, one of its deep curiosities is the marriage stone in the heart of the island. It has a hole in the lower part through which couples who vow themselves to each other can touch hands. The origins of its tradition are unknown.

MARTYR

On the edge of Rathcormac village, opposite the old school, the site of the 'Hanging Trees' is marked. Three more modern trees occupy the site today.

On 16 June 1798, John Dahill and Nicholas Burke were court-martialled for encouraging and overseeing illegal oaths for the United Irishmen. Both were prosecuted, found guilty, sentenced to death and executed by hanging. It is said that Dahill's execution took place in nearby Curraglass. However, his body was then brought back to Rathcormac for burial because of his family roots.

Local folklore has it that Dahill's body was placed hanging on one of the trees in order to make an example of him to other locals joining the United Irishmen. On Dahill's headstone is inscribed his name and that he 'died a martyr'.

The local gentry took offence to the inscription on Dahill's headstone and got the words 'a martyr' chiselled out. This only had the knock-on effect of immortalising him even more among the local population. In 1998, to signify the bicentenary of the 1798 Rising and the legacy of the United Irishmen, Cork sculptor Ken Thompson restored the Dahill headstone to its original condition in the graveyard of the old Christ Church in Rathcormac.

MASSACRE

The formal unveiling of the Gortroe Massacre memorial stone took place on 16 December 1984. Sculpted by Michael Sheedy of Midleton, the memorial depicts two panels: one shows a young boy blowing a cow horn to summon the community to resist the troops as they come to collect tithes; the second shows the Widow Ryan, who owned the tithes. She is weeping by a stack of corn, the twelve ears of which represent the twelve who died at the massacre, which took place on 18 December 1834. It was where the last great fight of the Tithe War of 1831–38 occurred.

Tithes were initially voluntary offerings to the Protestant clergy in appreciation for their work. They were separated into three sums, one of which was to deliver education for all the poor and for the youth of the parish; the second was for the needs of the impoverished and the sorrowing and the hungry; the third was to provide for the upkeep of the local Protestant church. The true opposition to the payment of tithes came with the Reformation when the clergy, becoming Protestant, were separated from the people.

Occupiers of land were obliged to pay tithes to clergymen whose services they rejected. After the passing of Catholic Emancipation in 1829, the public turned towards getting rid of the tithes, which were levied on crops and not on grassland and thus affected the hard-working farmer.

The house of Widow Ryan of Gortroe townland stood on a hill overlooking the road from Rathcormac to Midleton. She owed £2 8s tithe to Rev. William Ryder and had refused to pay it in protest against the tithe system and in agreement with her neighbours.

On the morning of 18 December 1834, a company of 100 men with their officers – making in all 121-armed men – were instructed from Fermoy to Rathcormac to arrive at the Ryan house at 10.30 a.m. to meet Rev. William Ryder and Captain Collis. Nine cavalry from the 4th Dragoon Guards were to complement them.

On arrival at the Tallow Road, between Bartlemy and Bluebell Cross, the cavalry observed that a crowd of people had gathered. The Riot Act was read but the people did not disband. The troops had already fixed bayonets. Now they

The Gortroe memorial with local Fred Wilson, present day. (Kieran McCarthy)

were given instructions to 'prime and load' their musket guns. Having complied, the troops moved down the lane to Mrs Ryan's house, the cavalry going ahead. A cart had been drawn across the lane leading to the haggard (a large haystack adjacent to a house) and the people had assembled in the yard behind the cart. They brought sticks. Captain Sheppard moved up front with a detachment, who were ordered by Major Walter to charge.

The soldiers leapt up on the cart but were hurled back. Walter ordered a flanking attack and the soldiers tried to get over the haggard wall but these were also pushed back. The order to fire was then given, but the crowd, instead of scattering as was expected, closed in on the cart and the soldiers fired at the men still standing at the cart, brandishing their sticks. A trumpeter sounded the ceasefire. In all, sixty-seven shots had been fired and nine men were killed and seven seriously wounded. A memorial stands at Gortroe today in memory of those killed.

✳ ✳ ✳

On 29 June 1845, the Ballinhassig Massacre took place and is attributed to a body of Royal Irish Constabulary under the command of an officer by the name of Hodnett, who resided in Kinsale. Every year, Ballinhassig held a busy fair with over twenty refreshment booths and extra police brought in from nearby stations. When the business of the fair had been more or less concluded, a small public gathering began to demonstrate. They were taken into custody by the constabulary, but friends soon followed and rescued them.

Officer Hodnett separated his constabulary into three sections and asked them to approach the crowd from different sides, complete with firearms. A public stampede ensued, which ran at one of the sections located near the town cross. A woman came out of a house and fell, mortally wounded.

Anger followed and a body of men charged against the constabulary. The police fired a second volley. The firing ceased for a short time when the supply of bullets ran out. At the village cross a pool of blood could be seen. Five bodies lay at one spot. Seven men and women had been killed. Twenty others were seriously injured. There was no fallout for the constabulary, but the memory of the event lasted for many decades.

MASTER

The modern and colourful town of Dunmanway owes its foundation to Sir Richard Cox, Lord Chancellor of Ireland and Speaker in the British House of Lords, who came into control of this area in the seventeenth century. Up to his intervention, the English Crown had formed a colony there as a resting place for troops marching between Bandon and Bantry.

Cox was accorded approval to hold two annual fairs and a weekly market, and he also created a textile industry that, by the mid-eighteenth century, had an international reputation for its products. Annually, on 1 May, the town's spinning wheels and cloths were displayed for the prize of a coveted title 'Master Manufacturer' and a year's free rent.

By 1700, about thirty families lived in the town. Sir Richard also built the long bridge over the River Bandon, consisting of six arches. With the decline of the local textile industry in the early nineteenth century, new industries were introduced.

Samuel Lewis in his *Topographical Dictionary of Ireland* (1837) notes that the manufacture of linen continued to flourish for some years, but in his present there were very few looms at work. He observes:

Since 1810 a considerable trade in corn has been carried on ... A porter and ale brewery, established in 1831, produces 2600 barrels annually; there are also two tanyards and two boulting-mills, the latter capable of grinding annually 15,000 bags of flour, and there are two or three smaller mills in the vicinity.

Lewis also points to one long street extending almost a kilmometre to the west of the bridge and describes that in 1831 it contained 419 houses, which, though 'indifferently built, are distinguished by an appearance of cleanliness and comfort'. Lewis also lists a market house, police station, dispensary, manorial court, a Church of Ireland and Roman Catholic chapel in the progress of erection, and a space for worship for Wesleyan Methodists.

It is said that Dunmanway derived its name from its Irish *Dúnmaonmhuí*, signifying 'the Castle of the Yellow River' or 'the Castle on the Little Plain', from an ancient castle belonging to the Gaelic clan of McCarthys.

MINE

Much is written about Mount Gabriel, on the Mizen Peninsula of west Cork, which hosts an assemblage of early Bronze Age copper mines. In the period between 1700 and 1400 BC, Mount Gabriel hosted Bronze Age miners who searched for copper deposits to smelt with tin so that they could create bronze tools and weapons.

Scholars relate that such copper mining was one of the earliest in north-west Europe. Several excavations were pursued on Mount Gabriel during the 1980s. They revealed that through the use of fire and stone hammers, the community of miners dug over thirty shafts into the hillside.

In the early nineteenth century, mining commenced again on Mount Gabriel and a new copper mine was opened at Coosheen, on the eastern side of the mountain overlooking Schull Harbour. This small mine was famous for barytes, which was utilised as a paint additive and in the production of paper. It was operated by Captain Thomas between 1839 and 1877 and was renowned for the richness of its deposits.

Late-nineteenth-century mine shaft overlooking Eyeries, Beara Peninsula.
(Kieran McCarthy)

MONSTER

Entering Gougane Barra Island, an information panel shows a winged dragon.
St Finbarr is said to have battled with a winged dragon named Lua – which
St Patrick had forgotten – that dwelt within Gougane Barra Lake. Legend has
it that Finbarr chased the serpent out of Gougane Barra. The serpent is said to
have woven down the Lee Valley and out to sea. The legend is remembered in
the valley's Lough Allua between Ballingeary and Inchigeela.

The dragon was represented at the opening ceremony of Cork's tenure as
European Capital of Culture in 2005, which used the myth to connect the city's
cultural heritage into the wider Cork region. In the north channel of the River
Lee in Cork city, a large puppet-like snake over 1,000m long was extended, over
which fireworks were launched.

Similar folklore is recalled at sites associated with Ireland's national saint,
Patrick. At Glendalough, St Kevin is remembered as driving a serpent out of
the local lakes and then establishing his monastery on the lakeside, where two
rivers meet.

MOONLIGHTING

A sharp decline in butter prices between 1877 and 1879 resulted in tenants finding it difficult to pay the same rent but many did so without complaint. However, violence grew and was directed at those who co-operated with the landlord system: land grabbers, caretakers of evicted farms and grazing grabbers or persons who hired grazing land on evicted farms.

On 29 December 1881, Macroom Police, acting on secret information, captured a discharged British Army soldier named Dan Connell in a farmer's house at Mushera, midway between Macroom and Millstreet. Connell was the main ringleader of the Millstreet Moonlighters. All were sworn members of a body calling itself the 'Royal Irish Republic'. Some of them wore military-style uniforms and carried military ranks. Drilling exercises were also performed and organised by Connell at Coolykeerane near Millstreet.

Documents also found in Connell's possession at the time of his capture revealed a highly organised group, with the 'Republic' acting as jury, judge and executioner whenever the unwritten agrarian code was violated. After his arrest, Connell became an informer and supplied the police with the names of his associates.

With the acquired list of culprits, the police arrested and charged forty-six persons with treason by March 1882. The arrest period revealed that the Moonlighters were the sons of farmers, small farmers, labourers and tradesmen and one assistant national school teacher. However, even with the 'Royal Irish Republic' disbanded, secret organised groups remained in operation across County Cork.

MOVIE

On 11 May 1954, a spokesman at London's Elstree Film Studios announced that John Huston and actor Gregory Peck would arrive in Youghal to film sequences for Huston's latest film, *Moby Dick*, as soon as other scenes being shot in Madeira were completed. A converted schooner was be sailed from Britain to be 'disguised' as the whaler ship *Pequod*, which features in the story. Youghal was chosen because of its resemblance to New Bedford, Massachusetts, from which *Pequod* sailed in search of the great white whale.

The decision to film some of *Moby Dick* in Youghal caused huge excitement with thousands flocking by car, train and bicycle to the seaside town to catch a glimpse of Peck, who played the obsessive Captain Ahab, and the rest of the cast.

By late June 1954, the time to start filming *Moby Dick* was coming nearer, and an ever-increasing activity was evident at the Market Dock area, where the filming was to take place. Cork Harbour Board's dredger was removing the silt from the dock.

Once filming began, every day, large numbers of people flocked to the dock. They had close-ups of all the actors and watched how Huston controlled and directed operations on this artificial busy quayside complete with busy stores, warehouses and barrels of whale oil.

During July 1954, the scenes needed were filmed. By the end of the month, demolition squads removed the beautiful artificial houses and the cobbled streets on the road to the docks as well as to the taverns, 'Spouter Inn' and 'Moby Dick Saloon'.

A 2020 statue by artist Matthew Thompson remembering the shooting of the film *Moby Dick* in Youghal in 1954. (Kieran McCarthy)

In August 2020, the Mayor of the County of Cork, Cllr Mary Linehan Foley, unveiled a sculpture in Youghal to honour the filming of *Moby Dick*. Cloyne-based artist Matthew Thompson designed and developed the sculpture. It was funded by Cork County Council, the Department of Rural and Community Development's Town and Village Renewal Scheme and by the fundraising endeavours of local community group Youghal 4 All.

MURDER

On 22 August 1922, Michael Collins, Major General of the Irish National Army, was assassinated at Béal na Bláth, County Cork. Collins and his party left Cork city at approximately 6 a.m. that morning, on a tour of west Cork. At approximately 8 p.m., on their return journey to Cork city through a valley, the party was ambushed by Anti-Treaty Forces, who had a roadblock in place.

A very insightful section in an RTÉ documentary in 1978, entitled *Emmet Dalton Remembers*, covered the life and times of Collins' right-hand man.

The programme at the point of writing is posted on YouTube. Dalton, at 80 years of age, was interviewed at Béal na Bláth.

He recalls that once the ambush started, he and Collins got out of their touring car and some fellow soldiers got off their Crossley tender and they hid behind a small ditch. It gave them cover from the angle from which the firing was coming, which was up from around 200 yards. Dalton recalls, 'From the volume that was there, I would say that there were but a half a dozen at the most – firing rifles. A chosen ambush position is always perilous, and this was obviously a very bad position. There was no area for retreat.'

With one eye on Collins and after ten minutes of engagement, Dalton witnessed Collins getting up and moving to the back of the armoured car. He used it as protection to have a better sight of what was happening on the hill above. Then he moved from there up around the bend, out of Dalton's vision, but he was firing from up ahead.

Dalton recalls that he thought he heard some of his convoy calling him:

I jumped up on at that stage. O'Connell had been up the road to me and he said where's the Big Fella, so I said he's around the corner around the bend. We both went up there and he had been shot. He was lying there with a very gaping wound to the back of his head. So I called the armoured car back and we lifted him and took him onto the side of the armoured car, we moved behind the armoured car with the armoured car between us and their firing position.

They got Collins to the position on the side of the road. Under protection of the armoured car, Emmet Dalton bandaged the wound and O'Connell said an act of contrition to him. They knew he was dying, if not already dead, so they did the best they could to cover up the wound. All action at this stage had practically stopped. They moved Collins' body onto the touring car.

Dalton sat in and carried Collins' weight on his shoulder in the car and they drove off back towards their home base of Cork. To this day, there is no consensus as to who fired the fatal shot.

MYSTERY

The story of the liner *Lusitania*'s sinking off the Old Head of Kinsale remains one of the world's greatest maritime mysteries. On 7 May 1917, the ship, which had travelled from New York, was bound to dock in Liverpool that afternoon.

On board there were 1,266 passengers and a crew of 696. At approximately 18km off the Old Head, she encountered a U-boat (*U-20*) at 2.10 p.m.

The commanding officer of the U-boat, Walter Schwieger, gave instructions to engage and to fire one torpedo, which hit *Lusitania* on the starboard bow. A short few seconds later, a second explosion was seen from the first hit spot within the ship's hull. The ship was seriously damaged and listed significantly to starboard.

The crew launched the lifeboats but the stark tilt made their task very difficult. Of the forty-eight lifeboats only six were launched with success. Many of them just overturned or broke apart. Just eighteen minutes after the first torpedo, the ship went under. Within a few short minutes, the masts and funnels disappeared beneath the ocean. Sadly, of the 1,962 passengers and crew, 1,198 people lost their lives during the sinking. Those who survived were down to the rescue crews who came to assist.

International outrage ensued. It was a British ship. As well as that, 128 out of 139 US citizens died. Much has been written about the ship and whether it was attacked illegally. Was it travelling in a neutral capacity? *Lusitania* was officially listed as an auxiliary warship and her cargo manifest openly detailed '4,200,000 rounds of rifle cartridges, 1250 empty shell cases, and 18 cases of non-explosive fuzes'.

The assistant manager of the Cunard Line, Herman Winter, rejected the insinuation that the ship was carrying munitions. He did concede that she was carrying small-arms ammunition but outlined that she had been carrying such munitions as cargo for several years. Consecutive British governments have always claimed that there were no munitions on board.

Bernhard Dernburg, a German spokesman and a former German Colonial Secretary, argued that the ship was carrying what he described as 'contraband of war'. He further claimed that because she 'was classed as an auxiliary cruiser', Germany could claim the right to attack her irrespective of the many passengers on board.

The wreck of *Lusitania* was located on 6 October 1935, 18km south of the Old Head of Kinsale lighthouse in roughly 93m of water. Over the decades, there have been many attempts to dive down to the wreckage. But it is a difficult process. Mixed gases must be used to dive down. As well as that, divers have also discovered a myriad of British depth charges and hedgehog mines. Sediment and fishing nets limit visibility. However, in September 2008, .303 cartridges of a type known to be used by the British military were recovered from the wreck by diver Eoin McGarry.

Lusitania's sinking remains a mystery. Check out the impressive art installation at the old watch tower at the entrance to the Old Head. It is the part of the scenic trail of the Wild Atlantic Way in the area.

NATION

Thomas Davis was born in the town of Mallow in 1814. He studied at Trinity College, Dublin, and received an arts degree, precursory to his being called to the Irish Bar in 1838. He established *The Nation* newspaper with Charles Gavan Duffy and John Blake Dillon. He dedicated his life to Irish nationalism. Thomas wrote some stirring nationalistic ballads, originally contributed to *The Nation* and afterwards republished as *Spirit of the Nation*. He was a Protestant but preached peace between Catholics and Protestants.

Thomas Davis was to the fore of Irish nationalist thinking and it was noted by later nationalist heroes, such as Padraig Pearse, that while Wolfe Tone laid out the basic fact that Ireland as a nation must be free, Davis was the one who built this idea up by promoting the Irish identity. He is the author of the famous Irish rebel song 'A Nation Once Again'.

Thomas died at the age of 30 in 1845. A statue of him, created by Edward Delaney, was unveiled on College Green, Dublin, in 1966.

NATIONALITY

Born in Castlecor, County Longford, in 1824, Thomas Croke was educated in Charleville in north Cork and in the Irish College in Paris. He was ordained a priest of the Catholic Church in 1846. Fr Croke fought on the barricades in Paris during the 1848 Revolution. He returned to Ireland where, in 1858, he became President of St Colman's College in Fermoy, County Cork, and later, he became the parish priest of Doneraile in 1865. Fr Croke attended the First Vatican Council as the theologian to the Bishop of Cloyne in 1870. In the same year, he was appointed second Bishop of Auckland, New Zealand. Bishop Croke became a member of the Irish hierarchy when he became Archbishop of Cashel, one of the four Catholic Irish archbishoprics, in 1875.

Portrait of Thomas Davis.
(Cork City Library)

Archbishop Thomas Croke was a strong supporter of Irish nationalism, aligning himself with the Land League and the Chairman of the Irish Parliamentary Party, Charles Stewart Parnell. He also associated himself with the temperance movement of Fr Theobald Matthew, the Gaelic League from its foundation in 1893, and the National Gaelic Athletic Association (GAA). He died in 1902. In honour of Archbishop Croke, his successors, as Archbishops of Cashel and Emly, traditionally are asked to throw in the ball at the minor Gaelic football and hurling All-Ireland finals at Croke Park, Dublin.

NEUTRAL

At the sharp cliff face of Toe Head in west Cork lies a historic Éire sign. Between 1943 and 1944, in the midst of Ireland's neutrality in the Second World War, eighty-three 'Éire' neutral signs were embedded into the Irish coastline, especially on headlands, by the Irish Government. They were requested from American forces. To make the signs noticeable to pilots, they were composed of the local rock, cemented into place and whitewashed. They had to be a regular size of 12m by 6m bordered by a broad rectangular edge.

The signs were located near to Look-Out Posts (LOP) and before long, again at the request of the US Air Force, the number of the relevant LOP was added adjacent to the sign. Such signs reiterated Ireland's neutrality but also aided American pilots in navigating their way around the Irish coastline.

The numbers added to the signs became handy navigational aids. A map of the numbered LOP was then presented to Allied pilots so that the signs could be employed to discover their course if they became lost or confused. This was an attempt to try and reduce the number of crash landings in Ireland. Despite these, sixteen crashes still occurred.

After the end of the Second World War, many of the signs became overgrown and neglected. Some were farmed over. Of the eighty-three signs created, however, thirty remain complete, including that on Toe Head. Just a few have been reinstated to their previous visible form.

NEWSPAPER

The legendary *Skibbereen Eagle* newspaper was founded in 1857 in Skibbereen. It began as a monthly publication and then became weekly. It took a British imperialistic stance on local, national and international affairs and it was aimed at the local Protestant land-owning and merchant classes. In the late nineteenth century, Skibbereen was also a busy commercial hub with steamship services and two railway lines – the Cork, Bandon & South Coast Railway and the narrow-gauge Schull & Skibbereen Railway.

The newspaper made global news when it began, as it noted in 1899, 'keeping an eye on Russia'. The editorial proclaimed of liberty and justice:

> It [the *Eagle*] will still keep its eye on the Emperor of Russia and all such despotic enemies – whether at home or abroad – of human progression and man's natural rights which undoubtedly include a nation's right to self-government. 'Truth', 'Liberty', 'Justice' and the 'Land for the People' are the solid foundations on which the Eagle's policy is based.

The intrepid editor and proprietor Frederick Potter printed a report on a secret treaty by Russia to extend its territory into the Muslim lands of the Caucasus in a violent operation spearheaded by the Cossack Cavalry. This phrase became famous and was referenced by European newspapers over the ensuing several decades. The *Skibbereen Eagle* newspaper was superseded by the *Southern Star* (established in 1889).

OLD

The story of Katherine Fitzgerald and her death at 140 years of age has embedded itself in County Cork folklore. The Countess of Desmond was the daughter of Thomas, 8th Earl of Desmond. She was born only a few weeks before her father was executed at Drogheda on a warrant from Edward IV, forged by the queen, who had sworn revenge on the earl for once suggesting to the king that he should never have married her.

After the earl's death, the king, irate at the tragic and pointless death of his old friend and comrade-in-arms, tried to make some recompence for his wife's betrayal by having the earl's baby daughter brought to court and reared and educated with his own children. Katherine grew up becoming a maid of honour to the queen.

In her mid-twenties, Katherine returned to Ireland, where she married her cousin, Sir Thomas Fitzgerald, of Inchiquin Castle near Youghal, a man far older than she was. The couple settled down at Inchiquin.

In 1529, the 11th Earl of Desmond died without an heir and Sir Thomas, who was his uncle and next of kin, inherited the Desmond title but died four years later. After his death, the countess, who was now 65, received the castle and lands of Inchiquin for her lifetime, and continued to live there with her daughter.

In 1579, the Earl of Desmond – Gerald Fitzgerald, from an Anglo-Norman family – was anti-English, and subsequently was stripped of all his estates including Inchiquin, leaving the unfortunate countess and her daughter homeless. She made up her mind to travel to London and demand justice from the king himself. She took a ship from Youghal to Bristol and when she arrived there, she purchased a handcart onto which she put her ailing daughter, then pushed her along in front of her as she walked all the way to London.

The king was by so impressed by the countess that he gave immediate orders for the castle and lands of Inchiquin to be restored to her for her lifetime, which he felt could not be very long. He then provided transport and an escort of soldiers to see her safely back to her old home, where, to everyone's amazement, she lived for another twenty-five years until her death in 1604.

A great many people have, from time to time, queried the age of the old countess, but the result of the research keeps coming back to 140 years of age!

ORIENTATION

Drombeg stone circle remains an enigma in the west Cork landscape. Lying just over 3km to the east of Glandore, every day, intrepid members of the public come to visit and walk around it. The stones look like parts of a big compass to help with orientation within the landscape. Archaeologist Edward Fahy literally put Drombeg on the map as the findings from his excavation of the site drew much media attention and were published in the eminent *Journal of the Cork Historical and Archaeological Society* in 1959. It was one of Edward's first excavations. He described the stone circle as a 'monument of great precision and refinement exhibiting the careful thought and planning which its builders put into its erection'.

Edward approached the study and excavation in meticulous detail. The monument before him comprised fourteen free-standing stones in a circular formation standing on a natural rock terrace. Such stones averaged 2m high, 1.10m wide and 45cm thick. A recumbent stone, an impressive flat-topped slab, stood in the south-western arc of the circle.

Edward and his team revealed through excavation that the inside of the circle possessed an unbroken, gravelled floor, 'in places 10cm thick, lying immediately below the 10cm of thick carpet of fibrous, soil-free turf within the circle'. The stones comprising the floor were mixed pebbles and flakes of slaty rock with sporadic lumps of quartzite.

Beneath the floor and almost in the centre of the circle, two pits were discovered – the larger held an 'inturned' cremation pot (6mm in thickness), while the smaller contained silt and stones and two other pits were full of shattered rock fragments.

The sockets of all the standing stones, or orthostats, were fully excavated. It was observed that they all more or less followed a consistent plan – closely rammed soil in the lower levels and boulders in the upper level. A small flint scraper was discovered in the top level of the fill of socket no. 10. A split flint pebble was found in a similar position in socket no. 15 and a small flint scraper was found above socket no. 7, but otherwise, the sockets of all stones were void of other material objects.

Excavation was pursued outside the monument and lengthened by trial trenches outward along the main axes of the site. No surrounding fosse, postholes or other features, other than the old turf line, outside of the circle, were revealed.

A second circle to the west was presented as a more extensive structure, which on excavation proved to be a stone hut. An extensive mound, south of the hut site, proved to be an intricate cooking place associated with the hut by a stone-built causeway.

Excavation work was also pursued on whether the recumbent stone aligned with the setting sun in midwinter. On 24 December 1957 and again on 23 December 1958, the setting sun was photographed by an independent observer, standing to the east of the portal stones, and was found to lie slightly south of the point

Winter solstice gathering at Drombeg Stone Circle, 21 December 2016. (Kieran McCarthy)

previously established as the axial intersection with the horizon. Edward Fahy argues in his journal article that the presence of trees on the horizon in former times would have altered the observed setting of the sun, that is to say that the sun would have set in a slightly more southern position than it did in the 1950s.

In his concluding comments in his journal article, Edward Fahy reflects he is unable to say what were the exact ritual ceremonies at Drombeg, but the dearth of scattered potsherds, broken implements or successive burials seems to signify that once the original dedication had taken place, the community, secure in the knowledge that the human remains of the cremated person were present within the circle, proceeded with their further ceremonies in such a manner that no material evidence of them was left in the soil.

OUTPOST

Completed in 1909, the first reinforced-concrete arched footbridge, at the geographical outpost that is Mizen Head, was built in the very early days of reinforced concrete and involved precast elements, composite construction and refined erection techniques. The initial intention of the bridge was to give access across dangerous cliff faces for the staff of the Commissioners of Irish Lights to the fog station at Mizen Head.

The designer was Noel Ridley AMICE and the system applied was patented in the name of Ridley and Cammell. The contractor was Alfred Thorne of Westminster, and the contract price was £1,272. Access at the time of assembly was by means of ladders attached to the cliff faces. The bridge was created using temporary suspension cables over a vast drop into the ocean.

Normal renovations were carried out on the bridge prior to the Second World War. However, in time, rust staining of the reinforcement became very distinct.

A unique type of anaerobic corrosion of the reinforcement was detected in 2004 and the bridge was closed for several weeks while a temporary scaffold was created. The duration of the temporary scaffold came to an end in 2009.

Construction work on the new bridge commenced in October 2009. This bridge is a replica of the existing reinforced-concrete structure and was constructed by forming a concrete mould (shuttering) into which reinforcement and ready mixed concrete was placed. The location of the bridge limited the sort of plant that could be used by the contractor. For example, it was not feasible to use a large crane or permit common construction vehicles at the bridge site. The majority of the works were carried out by hand and were labour intensive.

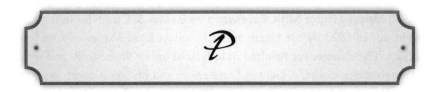

PAPER

Dripsey village, along the Lee Valley, began in the townland of lower Dripsey and grew with the development of paper mills by Jimmy Batt O'Sullivan of Dripsey. He was a well established and esteemed manufacturer in the last decades of the 1700s.

In the Irish context, there were approximately fifty paper mills in the country in the 1770s and '80s, and over 50 per cent of these were located in or near Dublin. In the 1750s, there were about six mills in southern Ireland, most of which were located in and around Cork city. The city provided the paper mills with a plentiful supply of rags from which waste fibres from the linen and cotton industries could also be used.

As a Roman Catholic, Jimmy Batt O'Sullivan benefited from the Catholic Relief Act of 1782, which permitted Catholics to purchase and inherit land and property. Jimmy soon became the largest paper manufacturer in the whole country, owning mills at Dripsey, Blarney, Beechmount, Towerbridge and Springhill. His exports were sent to England and comprised writing, printing, lapping and tea paper.

In the early years of operation, it is known that Jimmy invested £50,000 in his mills at Dripsey and Blarney in contemporary machinery. Much of the Dripsey paper was exported to England. The mill was the first to manufacture ruled paper. The sap of the red willow, a tree that grew in abundance on both banks of the River Dripsey, formed the main colour constituent of the formula Jimmy used for lining paper. Jimmy also devised a colouring process for the Bank of England notes made at Dripsey for the Treasury in London. In 1804, he was producing watermarked paper.

About the year 1812, Jimmy leased a farm of 207 acres at Agharinagh, just west of the mills, known as The Acres. Through his farming ventures, Jimmy became a member of the Royal Agricultural Society.

The economic downturn of the late 1810s, after the end of the Napoleonic Wars, resulted in O'Sullivan selling off Dripsey Mills and other industrial assets.

By 1817, Dripsey Paper Mills was owned by Reeves & Co., who in turn were bought out in 1823 by Sir Christopher Magnay, Lord Mayor of London in 1822–23. The changeover resulted in industrial unrest at the mills and serious damage to the machinery. George Stephenson and his son Robert, who both designed the first steam locomotives, visited Dripsey Paper Mills in 1823 to inspect the damage. The replacement parts were bought from Stephenson's Newcastle factory between December 1823 and August 1827.

In 1846, Mr Alfred Greer took over the Dripsey complex. At one time, it is said that about 400 people worked in Dripsey Paper Mills. That is a sizeable community, a large portion of who would have lived in the Dripsey area.

Dripsey Paper Mills continued to function for several years following 1861 and the death of Alfred Greer, when the factory was operated by his son, A. Greer. In Henry and Coughlan's *Directory of Cork* for 1867, the Greer warehouse was based at 10 and 11 Academy Street, Cork city, and was one of nine paper warehouses in the city. During the 1860s, British Government excise duty on the manufacture of paper strained the financial position of Dripsey Paper Mills. Shortly afterwards, during an overhaul of the plant, one of the heavy iron bearings was accidently broken. Sufficient capital was not available for the cost of replacement and so about 1880, the once flourishing company closed.

Up to the early 1950s, the buildings were partly standing. The old mill shaft was the only portion intact. It was a tower completely clad in ivy. The Lee Hydro Electric Scheme in the mid-1950s covered the entire site with water, immersing its history into the depths of Inniscarra Reservoir.

PENAL

The story of Gougane Barra, as a site of pilgrimage, emerges in essence with the arrival of a priest, Fr Denis O'Mahony, in the late seventeenth century. Through his creative and imaginative actions, he connected and embedded Finbarr to the source of the Lee and rooted his hagiography in early Christian times. In O'Brien's *Life of St Finbarr* (*c.* 1902), Fr O'Mahony countered the penal laws in Ireland through building a pilgrimage site, thus defying the laws himself and being part of a multitude of movements condemning the laws.

Fr O'Mahony created a set of contemplative cells, lodgings and a basic church, a place for the pilgrim to interact with and a key site of memory to St Finbarr. There are no known ruins recorded before O'Mahony's construction. In the 150 years following Fr O'Mahony's intervention in the landscape, the act of pilgrimage was reconstructed to have what could be coined a heavier memory weight in the national, public and indeed the local vernacular psyche.

The various acts of remembering were widened and reconstructed over several decades by Cork clerics and antiquarians. The name of the local townland, Dereenacusha, was replaced unofficially by the name Gougane Barra (translated as Finbarr's rocky cleft). In a modern sense, this provided a regional branding for the site and also embedded the saint's link in the region, while connecting it even further to a national perspective – that of a national hagiography of Irish saints.

The erection of an inscribed stone *c.*1824, at the base of the front of the pilgrimage cell structure, sets and lists the ritual via a rounds system of prayers to be completed around the pilgrimage island – a pathway around the small island, linking ideas and thoughts together about the different values offered by the place. Two principal pilgrimage days were also chosen for Gougane Barra, one on 23 June (St John's Eve) and the other on the saint's day on 25 September. The saint's day was remembered and celebrated on the nearest Sunday and became known as the Gougane Sunday ceremonies, which included Mass and rounds of prayers.

The appointment, *c.*1890, of a new parish priest, Fr Patrick Hurley, to Gougane Barra and its environs led to further 'reconstruction' and 'modification' and endowment of memory at the site. A learned man with an enormous interest in the resolution of social problems, he worked amidst the slums of Cork city for several years. He amassed a huge interest in Irish religious history, archaeology, identity and the Irish language, and noted in several published papers the revamp of the pilgrimage island as adding to the Gaelic revival process.

In 1901, Fr Hurley commissioned the building of St Finbarr's Oratory. Its architecture was modelled on St Cormac's Chapel in Cashel, County Tipperary, one of the icons of early Christian architecture in Ireland. Fr Hurley also commissioned the building up of the collapsed walls of the pilgrimage cells, the creation of new Stations of the Cross and the landscaping of a new graveyard space. He also commissioned a memorial in Gougane Barra to poet Joseph Callanan, who wrote a poem evoking the scenic nature of the site.

Around 3km north of Newmarket, there is a field and in the middle of this there is a tree known as the Chalice Tree. When this tree blooms each year the blossoms are of a rich, red colour. It has a long, straight stem and it is shaped like a chalice; therefore it gets the name from this.

Adjoining this field is a smaller one where two graves are to be seen and in it there grows a sycamore tree. The graves are said to be those of the two priests who were murdered during the penal laws. Up to the late 1920s, it is said that each Christmas night, candles and the form of a priest praying near the tree could be seen.

Local folklore indicates that before they were murdered the priests had hastily buried a chalice in a hole. The Chalice Tree grew up out of that hole. However, the tree has since been dated and is between 150 and 200 years old, but no older.

The chalice vanished after the priests were both murdered. Its story remains vague for over two centuries, until the chalice reappeared in the collections of the Victoria & Albert Museum in London. The museum bought the Mount Keefe Chalice from an heiress of a large country estate in Cork for £400 in 1929. It still lies in the museum's collections.

PETTICOAT

Petticoat Loose was a term synonymous with all that was ghostly and superstitious in County Cork and south Munster in the nineteenth century. The spirit is still spoken about in folklore in rural parts of the county. The legends of Petticoat Loose were most plentifully told by horse and carmen, or cartmen, of butter firkins, or barrels. The stories differed in many respects, but one thing they had in common was that all were agreed the apparition was evil.

It usually appeared in the guise of a woman who cut the ropes that bound the firkins of butter. It was known to shriek demoniacally as the firkins rolled about the road, especially when the night was pitch black or on the most rural and winding of roads. One such story has prevailed in folklore and is connected to an east Cork location.

Sometime in the late nineteenth century, a Cork man whose name was James was employed as a firkin transporter. In summer, his principal trade was in the carriage of butter. In spring and winter, his work was supplemented by any other work he could get to keep his men and horses employed.

In winter, James acquired a lucrative contract for the drawing of sand to the city. This necessitated his carts leaving Cork at night, reaching the seashore by dawn, then loading and returning to the city. The horses rested during the day and the carts with fresh horses and drivers were employed in normal work in the city. This schedule appeared very satisfactory in the beginning, but gradually fell apart. James, enquiring on the reasons, discovered the men had been terrified by apparitions at a certain part of the road on several occasions. The horses sensed the spirit as much as their drivers, as he could see from their condition when they arrived in the mornings.

After consideration, James decided that he would lead the expedition himself and the men agreed. Accordingly, after nightfall, they started. James, in the leading butt, had provided himself with a hazel wand, a bottle of holy water and his rosary beads.

Eventually, they arrived at the part of the road that was designated haunted and it certainly looked forbidding. On both sides were the high walls of a demesne, uninterrupted by gate or wicket. High trees shadowed the road, with the wind whistling through the bare branches.

Shortly after James had entered this part of the road, an object bounded onto the road in front of James' horse. It appeared to be a large black dog, blacker than the surrounding darkness. Where it had come from, James did not know. It stood on the road in front of the horse and bayed balefully. The horse trembled with fright. The dog soon disappeared; its place being taken by another, and larger, black like the first, with two red glowing eyes and a menacing growl. It caused the horses to rear and plunge and gave James and his men great difficulty in keeping them under control.

The larger dog also disappeared and the horses quietened down. James and his party moved on. They were coming towards the end of the gloomy avenue, when a huge hound as large as a mastiff appeared on the road and its menacing bay reverberated through the avenue, throwing the whole party into confusion. Horses reared and plunged, drivers leaped from their carts with mingled prayers and cries of terror, endeavouring again and again to restrain the terrified animals.

At this juncture, James saw fire upon the road, gradually getting larger and brighter. Such a fire as he had never before seen, bright red and blue rains alternating and lighting up the road with the three hounds, now silent.

In front of the fire stood a woman, the details of her dress and appearance becoming clearer at each moment. On the further side of the fire were a number of women, not so distinctly outlined. Hastily James drew a circle with his hazel rod round his horse and cart, sprinkling it with holy water. He stood within the circle and called on and continued praying until daylight, regardless of what he could see or hear.

The woman came towards James, stately and graceful, and with a voice sounding like the tinkling of a silver bell, invited him to come to her. But James remained solemnly silent, praying fervently. She approached nearer and although the voice sounded friendly and seductive, the expression in her face was the opposite.

At the same time, James raised his crucifix. She leapt backward; the smile was replaced by a distorted grimace of hate, and the silver voice changed to a strident scream of an old hag and three hounds. Behind James rose the steady, fervent murmur of prayer from his petrified men. James demanded she depart. She eventually did, as quickly as she had arrived.

PIRATE

The Sack of Baltimore is one of the most sensational episodes in Irish history. It occurred during the summer of 1631. The local population comprised settlers from England who were involved in the local pilchard fishery. Their presence was overseen by the local Irish Chieftain Sir Fineen O'Driscoll.

Local ships were always subject to local piracy but the Baltimore episode originated from foreign climes. From the Barbary Coast, Dutchman Murat Reis the Younger led two pirate ships made up of crews of Dutch, Algerian and Turkish descent. Along their way to the west Cork coastline, they had taken several smaller, defenceless ships, after which they imprisoned their crews. They also had their eyes out for defenceless villages and coastlines, where one could creep up by stealth on quiet villagers.

Before dawn on 20 June 1631, the Reis ships launched an attack on sleeping Baltimore. Two hundred armed pirates descended on the surprised villagers. They set the thatch of roofs on fire and targeted the young and old. Soon, the rest of the village was awake from the sounds of screams and musket guns. Reis ended his raid but not before he and his group drove their haul of captured villagers back to their ships.

By that time, more than 100 men, women and children had been taken. They were herded back to the ships, which bore them away from the coves of west Cork to the slave markets of north Africa. Three women were discovered on the Barbary Coast in a local Algiers slave auction, some years later, but the fate of the others remains unknown.

✳ ✳ ✳

Anne Bonny (also, Ann Bonny or Anne Bonney) was a famous female pirate in the Caribbean. She was born in County Cork in the late 1600s, the daughter of an attorney and his maid. The lawyer left Ireland in disgrace but found fortune in the Carolinas in North America. There, he amassed a fortune and bought a large plantation. Anne left her fortune behind and chose the high seas as a life. She sailed in the crew of pirate Calico Jack Rackham.

Anne fought in men's clothing, was an expert with pistol and cutlass and was considered as dangerous as any male pirate. She was often a member of the boarding party. In October of 1720, the Governor of Jamaica, hearing of Calico's presence, sent an armed sloop to intervene and capture the captain and crew. Calico's ship *Revenge* was caught by surprise and the pirates captured. Anne was captured but confessed her sex and 'pleaded her belly' (pleaded being pregnant). After being examined and found with child, Anne was sentenced to be hanged. She received several stays of execution before mysteriously vanishing from official records. The Disney film *Pirates of the Caribbean* is based on the above characters.

POISON

On the southern side of the older Church of Ireland ruins at Coachford lies the separate tomb of Mary Laura Cross. Born on 21 August 1840, she was the victim of the famous Dripsey poisoning case. Local historian Anthony Greene, in *The Coachford Record* for 1990, related that her husband was Philip Henry Eustace Cross, who was a surgeon-major in the English Army. He did service in the Far East, Africa and Canada. He married Mary (Mary Laura Marriott) in Piccadilly, London, in 1869. He was 44 and she was 28.

Returning to Canada, Mary had four children: Bob, Harry, Mona and Bess. The couple retired to Shandy Hall in Dripsey, County Cork, where the fifth child, Etta was born. The Cross family became members of the local gentry and were wealthy. Philip Cross had an army pension of £200 a year, ran a stud farm, was a cattle and sheep farmer and had a number of tenants. He had also inherited £5,000 from his father-in-law. His wife Mary had a small income from her brother and her father's will provided for ten yearly payments of £5,000.

In 1883, arising out of a dispute with a tenant, Philip Cross was boycotted by the local community. As a result, his stud business collapsed and his labourers left. By 1887, Mary had become depressed and over time began to fear that she was dying of heart failure. At this time, Philip began to develop a relationship with 21-year-old governess, Effie Skinner, who was based at the local Caulfield residence nearby.

Mary's condition deteriorated and on the night of 2 June 1887, she died in much pain. Dr Cross made out the death certificate, highlighting the cause of death was typhoid fever and that the duration of her illness was fourteen days. She was buried in the Magourney Church of Ireland graveyard. Philip went to London to see his children. There also he met Effie Skinner, who at this stage was three months pregnant. Returning to Shandy Hall alone, rumours abounded with stories of the affair and that maybe Philip had killed Mary.

The rumours escalated and were taken seriously by District Inspector Tyacke of Ballincollig Royal Irish Constabulary, who wrote to the local coroner requesting that the body of Mary Cross be exhumed. In the presence of a Dr Crowley and Dr Charles Yeverton Pearson, lecturer in Medical Jurisprudence at Queen's College (now University College Cork), the body was dug up and taken to the courthouse, where an inquest began. Small parts of the body were taken for scientific examination and Dr Pearson found traces of arsenic.

Dr Philip Cross was arrested and charged with the murder for his wife. He awaited trial in Cork Gaol. Several friends of the family and from the local Coachford area gave testimonies. The combined evidence found Cross guilty of murder and he was hanged on 10 January 1888.

PRISON

Between the parishes of Knockraha and Watergrasshill in mid-County Cork, around 200m above sea level, lies a place known as Rea. In the middle of its local cemetery at Kilquane, the local IRA unit utilised an old underground mausoleum during the Irish War of Independence in 1920 and 1921 to hold prisoners captured by Cork IRA Brigade No. 1 and who were subsequently executed.

Built of solid stone, the mausoleum had seemingly been used for hosting dead bodies to prevent happy-go-lucky body snatchers. For decades, the structure was covered with overgrowth and the historic fragments of shattered tombstones. Measuring 4.8m by 2.4m across and 1.8m high, beyond the entrance point was a set of six descending steps. At that point was a strong 6in steel door and gate that when closed made the interior of the mausoleum completely pitch dark.

The local IRA unit nicknamed their acquired prison 'Sing Sing' after the infamous New York correctional facility. They drilled holes in the steel door to provide ventilation and the vault was cleaned out. Research has revealed that at least thirty-five individuals were held at 'Sing Sing' and were subsequently executed.

Across 2012 and 2013, Knockraha Historical Society put their plans in place to refurbish and make this historic prison a visitable and accessible site to the general public. Today, it is still possible to view the holes in the iron door drilled by Ned Maloney, the local blacksmith and so-called 'Governor of Sing Sing'.

PROMISE

'Build me a castle. O I am no Judge of architecture; but it must be larger than any other house in Ireland and have an entrance tower to be named the White Knight's Tower. No Delay! It is time for me to enjoy.'

These words, uttered by George Kingston, kickstarted the architect brothers James and Richard Pain to design his great mansion ahead of a promise by his friend, George IV, to visit the Kingston home in Mitchelstown on his next Irish excursion. In 1823, construction was ready to go. The older Palladian home on the site was taken down, which itself was built on the site of an earlier castle. The new eighty-bedroom home atop a hill also had three libraries, a dining room, a morning room and a drawing room as well as state apartments, which included a long gallery.

Samuel Lewis, in his *Topographical Dictionary of Ireland* in 1837, remarked of the stately home and its lavish exterior and interior:

> The buildings occupy three sides of a quadrangle, the fourth being occupied by a terrace, under which are various offices: the principal entrance, on the eastern range, is flanked by two lofty square towers rising to the height of 106 feet ... The entrance hall opens into a stately hall or gallery, 80 feet in length, with an elaborately groined roof, richly ornamented with fine tracery, and furnished with elegant stoves of bronze, and with figures of warriors armed cap-à-pie; at the further extremity is the grand staircase. Parallel with the gallery, and forming the south front and principal range, are the dining and drawing-rooms, both noble apartments superbly fitted up and opening into the library, which is between them: the whole pile has a character of stately baronial magnificence, and from its great extent and elevation forms a conspicuous feature in the surrounding scenery.

A designed landscape, or demesne, surrounded the new house. The house and demesne was surrounded by a high stone wall enclosing 500 hectares, which were retained as the private grounds of the King family. Samuel Lewis further relates that the demesne was embellished with 'luxuriant plantations', and included an old church and graveyard, farming establishment on an extensive scale, with buildings and offices of a superior description, costing £40,000. The entrance lodge was to be based on the model of Cork city's Blackrock Castle. It is estimated that the castle, with the conservatories, farm and the general improvement of the demesne, cost the Kingston family more than £200,000. Notable also was the creation by Lord Kingston of the nearby Kingston Square and College.

After all the work, though, George IV never returned to Ireland and his promise was not upheld. Lord Kingston also developed a mental illness. However, what was created was one of the finest neo-Gothic houses that Ireland has ever seen.

In June 1922, during the Irish Civil War, Republican Volunteers took control of the castle and evicted its owners. On 12 August 1922, the house was burned down. The ruins were taken apart and its ashlar limestone was sent to be used to construct a new Cistercian abbey at Mount Mellery, County Waterford. The historic Kingston site of the house is now occupied by Dairygold, one of the leading Irish agri-food companies. Across Mitchelstown are interpretative panels telling the story of the Kingston family's influence on the town.

T. Barber's engraving of Mitchelstown Castle, 1825. (Cork City Library)

QUAKE

In the early morning of 1 November 1755, a formidable earthquake physically and brutally shook the southern and western parts of Portugal. The earthquake was triggered along a large fault line that splits Europe from north Africa and was initiated almost 200km due south of Lisbon.

With an approximate intensity of 8.5 and 9 on the Richter scale, for nine minutes the earthquake persisted and comprised three separate jolts. A tsunami ensued, with several highly destructive waves which engulfed Lisbon. Wave heights varied between 6 and 30m along the Portuguese and Spanish coasts. Such was the intensity, the tsunami impact hit Brazil to the west, north Africa to the south and Britain and Ireland to the north.

On reaching west Cork and on Courtmacsherry Bay, the waves dragged sediments, sand and rocks and dumped such materials all across Timoleague Estuary, causing a ceasing of trade to Timoleague Abbey. As a result, a new docking area and village sprung up at Courtmacsherry. A number of high-profile sand dunes were also created at sites such as the Long Strand near Rosscarbery, the Warren Beach, and of course, Barley Cove near the Mizen Head. Check out University College Cork's Deep Maps online website and project and the section by Dr Kieran Hickey and Dr Anthony Beese for further information.

QUIRKY

The adventures of nineteenth-century north Cork man and returning emigrant Johnny Roche could be described as very quirky. In the immediate years after Ireland's Great Famine, he built a tower house on the bank of the River Awbeg (now a ruin). He called it Castle Curious and located it near Castletownroche in north Cork.

It is said that the three-storey limestone tower was built by hand and by John himself. He sourced lime from Mallow, stone from nearby quarries and took sand from the adjacent river.

John's eccentricities are still discussed to the present day. He physically blew a horn from the top of the turret. He tailored his own clothes, made his own buttons, made and fixed fiddles and musical pipes. He also constructed a mill for flannels and showed expertise in blacksmithing to dentistry. One story related that he manufactured false teeth from the hooves of cows.

Johnny Roche even planned his own resting place, an elaborate tomb in the adjoining Awbeg River. However, when he died in 1884 he was not buried there but still penned his own epitaph: 'Here lies the body of poor John Roche, he had his faults but don't reproach; For when alive his heart was mellow, an artist, genius and comic fellow.'

Barley Cove, present day. (Kieran McCarthy)

RADAR

Across 1974 and 1975 an aircraft control station was built on Mount Gabriel, which overlooks Schull and Roaringwater Bay. It was built for the European Organisation for the Safety of Air Navigation (Euro Control for short), whose headquarters were in Brussels and for which the Ministry of Transport and Power was the agent in Ireland with Aer Rianta (the Irish Airport Authority) acting as building consultants. The station was to use radar to monitor aircraft approaching the coast for their speed, direction, altitude and type, transmitting the data automatically by radio link through to London and Shannon, where it was needed for the safe routing of international air traffic. A similar station became operational at Woodcock Hill in County Clare to monitor the north-western sector of Ireland.

With Ascon Ltd of Dublin as the building contractors, the work began in June 1974 and included the building of about 2km of road, which partly follows the old track to the disused mines on the northern side of the mountain. The job involved the excavation of 20,000 cubic yards of rock and half as much bogland, and required 22,000 tons of imported gravel for filling.

The site consists of a fenced-off area on top of the mountain. It included two circular two-storey buildings, 9.1m in diameter and similar in construction, with a single-storey annex for generators and ancillary equipment. One of them was sleeping quarters and a kitchen for the small team who would man the station. The buildings had to be designed to withstand winds of up to 200mph, and were constructed with double cavity walls, the outside being faced with brick. Resistance to rain and fog, as the inclement hazards of Mount Gabriel, was another important consideration.

The 12.1m diameter domes (radomes, as they are called) to house the radar equipment were fitted on top of these 7.3m-high buildings. In 1982, the National Liberation Army blew up one of the domes as they believed it was a NATO installation, which would have indicated a violation of Irish neutrality. The dome was subsequently rebuilt. Both domes are still in operation.

One of the radar domes or 'radomes' atop Mount Gabriel, Schull, present day. (Kieran McCarthy).

RAID

Seán O'Driscoll, of Schull Battalion, Cork IRA III Brigade, remembers a most fascinating raid on Fastnet Rock lighthouse, perhaps the bravest of all the raids on British gun stores during the Irish War of Independence in Cork. It occurred in mid-June 1921 and is recorded in depth in his witness statement in the Bureau of Military History (reference: WS1518).

Seán explains that explosives were critically needed at the time for the manufacture of mines. They were challenging to acquire as the British were keeping their supplies in lighthouses along the coast, due to the fact they were difficult places to raid. Seán recalls that local fishermen were very helpful with information on how to access such lighthouses safely:

> Local fishermen kept us informed as to the quantities and times that gun cotton was stored in the Fastnet. Seán Lehane, the Officer in Command, decided that the lighthouse must be raided and a supply of explosives obtained. With the co-operation of the Schull and Cape Clear fishermen, we Seán Lehane, Jim Hayes and I planned a raid on the lighthouse. The Schull battalion planned to carry out the raid on a Saturday night or early Sunday morning, which stands about 3 miles south-west of Cape Clear and some 12 miles from the mainland.

John O'Regan, the proprietor of the Pier Road Hotel, Schull, who knew the geography of the south-west coast well, was to operate the boat and attempt a landing. At about 5 p.m. one Saturday evening, John, with William Daly, in a motor boat owned by William Cadogan, picked up Seán Lehane, Jim Hayes and Seán at Long Island point and set out for Cape Clear.

Poor weather postponed the first attempt. John O'Regan and William Daly returned to Leamcon near Schull, while Seán Lehane, Jim Hayes and Seán went ashore Cape Clear. At about the same time on Sunday evening, John O'Regan, William Daly, Michael Murphy (Gunpoint), Tim Murphy (Colla) and Charlie Cotter (Schull) also landed on Cape Clear.

A British destroyer stationed at Crookhaven was circling the Fastnet Rock Lighthouse. It was decided that, if challenged, they would pretend that we were fishermen. Indeed, of the eleven men who undertook the raid, seven were actually fishermen. The mail boat, named the Máire Cáit, belonging to Tadhg O'Regan of Cape Clear, was requisitioned for the job.

On the island (Cape Clear) this party was joined by Seán Lehane, Jim Hayes, Seán O'Driscoll witness and three islanders, Dan O'Driscoll, Dan Leonard and Dan Daly. Seán continues the story of the daring raid:

> As the June sun tipped the rim of the horizon, John O'Regan took the Máire Cáit out of the North Harbour, swung her north-west, then westwards, steering into a flaring sunset. Up from the south came the destroyer, her grey bulkheads plunging through a golden sea, a plume of white foam in her wake. The destroyer passed, heading for Crookhaven and soon disappeared into the half-light that followed the sinking of the sun.
>
> After midnight the boat approached the lighthouse. Moonlight flooded the somewhat calm sea. As the boat came nearer, rising and falling with the heaving of the sea, poised on the bow was John O'Regan, a rope tied to his waist, and a revolver in his pocket. It was his job to jump on to the landing platform. He had to time his leap.

John O'Regan jumped, the rope trailing behind him, and landed on the concrete space before the huge door of the lighthouse. In a split second he was pulling at the rope, bringing the boat into the rock. When the boat reached the rock they all got onto the platform. The steel door of the lighthouse was open.

John led the way up the circular stairway to the light room, where they held up the lighthouse keeper on duty and informed him that they had come for the gun cotton. Seán recalls the round-up of the lighthouse keepers:

The other two keepers were then rounded up and they removed the gun cotton and detonators from the stores. In all, the raiding battalion took away seventeen boxes of gun cotton and three boxes of detonators. They were all swung from the lighthouse on to the boat below. In about half an hour the battalion made their way in the Máire Cáit to Leamcon near Schull Harbour.

As the boat entered Long Island channel the lights of the British destroyer appeared astern. There was a momentary flutter of excitement. The lights disappeared and fifteen minutes later the spoils from the lighthouse were safe on shore.

The next day, gun cotton was distributed to units throughout the Cork III Brigade.

RELAX

The historic Spa House is clearly embedded in the life and culture of Mallow. Its history dates back to early Christian times, where tradition has it that the well was dedicated to St Patrick. When a charter was granted by King James in 1688, to David Miagh, Provost, he described at that time: 'Near the Spaw there are pleasant walks agreeably planted and on each side are canals and cascades, for the amusement and exercise of the company who have music on these walks.'

The commencing of the promotion in 1724 of the curative powers of the Mallow Spa made it quickly become one of the chief holiday resorts of Ireland well into the late nineteenth century.

In 1776, Arthur Young described the spa of that time as 'a small canal with walks on each side leading to the Spring under cover of some very noble poplars'.

Samuel Lewis, in 1837, noted that the approach to the spa from the town was partly through an avenue of lofty trees along the bank of an artificial canal 'affording some picturesque scenery'. The water of the spa had a mean temperature of 70°F, rising in summer to 72° and falling in winter to 68°. Lewis considered it as a 'powerful restorative to debilitated constitutions and peculiarly efficacious in scrofulous and consumptive cases'. The visitation season to the spa usually began in May and finished at the beginning of October, during which period there was a considerable influx of people who boosted the coffers of nearby lodging houses.

In 1828, the Spa House was built by C.D.O. Jephson, MP, the lord of the manor and principal proprietor of Mallow town. Samuel Lewis describes that the building was in the old 'English style of rural architecture' and contained a small pump room, an apartment for medical consultation, a reading room and baths. It supplied to its clientele hot and cold salt water, vapour and medicated baths.

* * *

The Royal Victoria Hotel and Baths at Glenbrook in Cork Harbour were immensely fashionable to visit during the mid-nineteenth century. Between June and October 1857, 15,000 bathers visited the establishment.

The hotel and baths were opened in 1838. The public were promised that the baths were 'finished in a manner equal, if not superior, to any baths in Europe' and 'the hot baths are composed of pure marble and the dressing rooms are fitted up in a style of great elegance, consisting of every comfort and luxury that can be required. Male and female domestics in constant attendance and every attention paid to invalids.' The advertisement also denotes that charges included 2d for a cold plunge, 6d for a cold shower and 15s for a dozen warm baths.

The growing popularity of Crosshaven as a new steamer ship traffic terminus within Cork Harbour and the opening of the Cork–Queenstown Railway in the 1860s gradually eroded business at the Glenbrook Baths, and after changing hands the premises finally closed around the turn of the twentieth century and fell into decay. All that remains is a section of wall next to what is now a children's play area.

REMEMBER

On 9 September 1887, William O'Brien, MP and national leader of the Land League, and John Mandeville were to be tried in court in Mitchelstown for what was deemed incitement to committing crime and for their role in leading the Kingston tenants in their battle against unfair rents on the Kingston Estate. After the court finished at 4 p.m., over 8,000 of their supporters, escorted by several brass and pipe bands, marched into the town's New Market Square, where they were to hear speeches from local leaders and Members of Parliament.

As the speeches began, thirteen members of the Royal Irish Constabulary (RIC) forced their way through the crowd. Many people protested and remained in the way of the police, thinking that they had come to arrest some of the speakers and prevent the meeting. Finding that their way was blocked, the police returned to barracks and came back with over fifty reinforcements, all armed with carbines.

Then the riot began, with RIC batons swinging and locals wielding blackthorns meeting the challenge, blow for blow. Eventually, the police were forced to retire and took refuge in the barracks round the corner, barricaded themselves in and prepared to protect themselves. Meanwhile, the victorious crowd had pursued the police and John Dillon, sensing what would happen, rushed to prevent them chasing the defeated police into the street where the barracks stood. He almost succeeded but some of the pursuers, including John Casey, were shot on the spot. John Shinnick and Michael Lonergan died a few days later from the effects of gunshot wounds.

There were many wounded, but they recovered. A great wave of furious indignation spread over the country. The incident was reported in the national newspapers of over fifty countries. On the following day, speaking in the Westminster Parliament, William E. Gladstone made the Mitchelstown murders one of his most powerful speeches. He coined the phrase 'Remember Mitchelstown'. He warned that before that watchword the Tory Government would fall. The Tories lost the next five by-elections in Britain and the Liberals used the Mitchelstown event to good political effect.

ROUTE

It was possibly the worst time to be a Surveyor of the Grand Jury in the East Riding of County Cork, or more or less the whole eastern side of County Cork, with Ballincollig as a central point. The Grand Jury, funded by Westminster, was a body comprising local landlords and magistrates. On 2 November 1853, an immense riverine flood carried away forty-six bridges in the district. By May 1854, County Surveyor Sir John Benson was reporting to the Grand Jury that he had prepared contracts for the rebuilding and repairing of twenty-four of them.

John Benson detailed in his report the complexities of not having bridges to cross rivers and the back-up of horses, carts and carriages:

> The destruction of so many important bridges have diverted in several cases the traffic on roads not prepared for such an increase, and consequently those roads are very much cut up. On some important thoroughfares the contracts have been taken at less than half the amount necessary for their maintenance – the consequence has been their almost total neglect by the contractors, and great inconvenience to the public.

John Benson could also boast having over 300km of roads added to the county in the previous eight years, which previously were repaired by private turnpike trustees. The additional cost to the Grand Jury would amount to £3,300 per annum, but the public would benefit from freedom from tolls.

ROW

The first rowing regatta was held on Inniscarra Reservoir in 1975. At that time, still and lake water coursing were becoming popular. In 1974, Shandon Boat and Rowing Club wished to mark its centenary the following year with something different from the norm. Mick O'Callaghan was captain of the club at the time. The organising committee were members who Mick had rowed with as a youth, John Cashell and Andy O'Connor. The senior member was vice- president Mick Collins. They laid out six lanes, 2,000m from Farran to the rowing centre at Rooves Bridge. Mick O'Callaghan recalls:

> We made a timber starting platform. The lanes were made of 12,000 metres of bailing twine and 700/800 one-gallon plastic containers, painted orange. Boats started from a platform made out of pallets, rope and concrete. The ESB [Electricity Supply Board] were very helpful, as were the local farmers at Rooves bridge. Mr McSwiney, the local farmer, gave us a section of his land for the day. We made slipways out of pallets.

In July 1976, the Home International Regatta was held over one day on Inniscarra Reservoir. It was an international rowing competition between Ireland, England, Scotland and Wales. On the second day, Shandon Boat Club held their annual regatta. During the 1980s and '90s, regattas were held intermittently on the reservoir.

There was no set plan – the Irish Championship was held on the reservoir, while club regattas took place over the former site of Inisleena Abbey. The Cork Regatta was held there once or twice. The Dripsey Channel held the Intervarsity College Rowing Championships, and UCC Rowing Club trained here also. In the early 1990s, the move to using multi-lane courses intensified – Cork City Regatta recognised the need for development and moved out to the reservoir in 1992.

In 1997, the Irish Championship was held on the reservoir, where it has taken place ever since. The European Junior Championships took place at Farran in 1999. In the late 1990s, Cospóir, the sport-development body in Ireland, wanted to upgrade international facilities and approached the National Rowing Union. Cork City Regatta Committee proposed the Farran venue, and a stretch of water was nominated on Inniscarra Reservoir and recommended by an international expert. It was deemed the best place to build the National Rowing Centre in the country.

SAGA

Ballycotton has seen almost 100 shipwrecks close to or off the coast of its shores between 1763 and 1996, with almost ten more near the shores of Ballycroneen. According to a report in the *Cork Examiner* on 19 February 1895, a Swedish brig ship called the *Saga* was discovered 'derelict', 'rudderless' and abandoned near Ballycroneen, between Poor Head and Ballycotton. It was believed the vessel had set sail for Central America from Burntisland, a parish in Fife, Scotland, at the beginning of January 1895.

On 12 March 1895, the goods recovered from the ship were sold by public auction. The various lots included thirty tins of paint, six cases of medicine and a few casks of linseed oil.

With nobody on board, nor any statement ever issued, the fate of the ship and her crew was an unresolved mystery until 2019 when Patricia O'Connell, who recovered the anchor of the *Saga*, undertook further research on the ship's history. With the help of local historians and records obtained in Stockholm and the Oskarshamn Maritime Museum in Sweden, Patricia solved the mystery and identified the wreck.

On 17 June 2021, the Mayor of the County of Cork, Cllr Mary Linehan Foley, unveiled the 126-year-old anchor from the *Saga* at Ballybrannigan Beach.

SCARECROW

It is a wonderful, scary experience to pass through the village of Leap at Halloween time. Since 2015, the village's annual scarecrow festival has been a must-see. Over 100 lifelike scarecrow creations of a wide variety of shapes and sizes are spread around the village. Chairperson Rita Ryan was initially motivated to create the festival after seeing figurines around the square in her native Thurles. A glance at the festival website highlights scarecrows such as 'a man built from branches brandishing a chainsaw, a Tim Burton-inspired Jack Skellington and his Corpse Bride, and a good witch and her pet cat'.

SEAWEED

At an early age, Ballylickey resident Ellen Hutchins, field botanist and plant hunter, developed a passion for natural history. Inspired by other botanists, Ellen took a deep interest in non-flowering plants called cryptogams, i.e. lichens, liverworts, mosses and seaweeds. She also gathered and studied shells.

By the age of 22, Ellen had discovered at least seven species new to science. She sent her plant specimens to botanists, who helped her publish her work. In addition, some of the plants were named after her by fellow botanists. She made a considerable impact on scientific knowledge as seaweeds were not well researched and understood at the time. Some specialists researching natural history argued that these might not be plants at all but sponges (which are animals). Ellen was the first botanist to assemble data of the fruit (fructifications) of one seaweed called Velvet Horn (*Fucus tomentosus*).

Ellen communicated eagerly with two botanists, Dawson Turner, in Great Yarmouth on the East Anglian coast of England, and James Townsend Mackay, at Trinity College Dublin. Several letters between Ellen and such botanists have survived, as well as some that she wrote to two of her brothers.

From 1808 onwards, Ellen also drew detailed watercolour drawings of the plants she was studying. The initial one was of Velvet Horn to illustrate its fructifications.

Dawson Turner had them engraved and used some of them as plates in his books and some in works by other botanists. Dawson asked Ellen to compile an extensive list of all the plants she could locate in her neighbourhood. It took three years for Ellen to compile such work and she listed over 1,000 plants, from trees to lichens. In one of her letters, she outlined that some of her days' work in the mountains began at 3 a.m.

Intervals of poor health hampered Ellen's passionate work and sometimes she could not go outside her house to explore for several months. Ellen was also the main carer for her mother, who was in poor health, and her disabled brother, Tom.

After a long episode of illness, Ellen died in 1815 at the age of 29. She was buried in an unmarked grave in Bantry's old Garryvurcha Churchyard. A plaque at her graveside now commemorates her work. The Ellen Hutchins Festival was established in 2015 to mark the bicentenary of Ellen's death. The annual festival hosts a wide variety of events, from walks to talks to workshops on Bantry Bay's natural and cultural heritage.

SHRIEK

In summer months, the little seaside spot of Robert's Cove near Carrigaline does not look at all like the scene of a most terrible tragedy of the sea. About 7 p.m. on the evening of 22 December 1775, the inhabitants of the district were horrified to hear moans and shrieks coming from the shore. Being superstitious folk, they drew down their window blinds, and in the morning the shrieks were explained in a most tragic manner.

The beach was strewn with wreckage and the horribly mutilated bodies of soldiers. A transport from Portsmouth – the *Marquis of Rockinghamshire* – with three companies of soldiers, along with two women and children, had been driven on the rocks by the heavy gale of the previous night and dashed to pieces. All on board, with the exception of three officers and thirty privates, had perished in the quiet little bay. Even those who had been saved had their flesh torn by the rocks, and to add to their horrors, they were attacked by several of the inhabitants, who carried off goods and personal possessions that could be saved.

SLAYER

In the heart of Donoughmore, legend tells of an event one Sunday morning with a small congregation who knelt in prayer before an outlawed priest in a field below a Mass rock at Ballyshoneen townland. It was the time of the penal laws and Roman Catholic Mass was outlawed.

On that day, a group of British soldiers under a Captain Fox – a priest slayer of sorts – made their way from the city to the Mass rock. On approaching the Mass, a thick fog prevented those attending seeing the arrival of Fox and his men.

It is said that Captain Fox stealthily made his way up behind the priest and cut his arms and head off. Fox then impaled the head on his sword. The congregation fled in terror across the landscape. Galloping after them, Fox's horse shied at a wall and Fox was thrown to the ground. He broke his neck and died from his injuries.

The soldiers with Fox panicked and quickly buried their captain in the graveyard of a small church near Loughane. Then they retreated to the city for fear of any reprisals by local people.

The legend does not end there. At midnight that night, the shallow graves of Loughane Graveyard, in which the dead were buried, began to tremble and move and the dead themselves broke through their earthen burials. Legend recalls that the entire graveyard awoke and moved their headstone across a field and up a hill to

Matehy Cemetery, where they reinterred themselves. Back in Loughane, a lone large flagstone marked the location of the graveyard and the burial place of Fox.

The graveyard and the small neighbourhood of houses are, to this day, identified by the Irish place name Magh Teithe, which literally means 'the Plain of the Fleeing from the Priest Murderer'.

SMUGGLE

In the eighteenth century, smuggling was apparently a thriving business along the rugged Cork coast, and there remain many old mansions that at one time played an active role in the contraband trade. Walton Court, which was a solid stone structure built in 1776, stood on a slope overlooking the picturesque bay of Oysterhaven.

Apart from its fame as a smugglers' headquarters, the house had other features that made it unique. It contained a remarkable little chapel on the ground floor in which a service was never held. The chapel, which must have one of the smallest in the world (it measures 3.6m by 7.3m), was installed in a ground-floor room by the clergyman tenant, who at the time was rector of a number of churches in the district. He purchased two large stained-glass windows, but in order to erect them the low ceiling had to be cut away in places. A plan to have an organ on the overhead floor was never carried out. The project, though obviously a sincere effort to cater for the needs of the local Protestant population, did not prove acceptable to the Church authorities and, consequently, no service was ever held there.

It is also said that the original owner, Thomas Walton, did an extensive trade in contraband goods, particularly silks and brandy, with France. For this purpose, there was apparently an underground passage running from the house to the beach some hundreds of yards below.

SOUND

High in the walls of the chancel of St Mary's Church, Youghal, are openings surrounding earthenware jars. Each jar is sitting on its side with the mouth facing into the chancel. The jars were positioned in the wall to enhance the acoustics of the church by inducing sound waves. The idea dates back to ancient Greek and Roman times.

Reconstruction of earthenware jars to improve acoustics in St Mary's Church, Youghal, present day. (Kieran McCarthy)

STORE

Born at Kilcanway, Killavullen, William Roche was educated locally and was apprenticed to the drapery trade with Cash's of Cork for five years. Having made several attempts to establish himself in business, he spent some years in England before returning to Cork in 1901.

William established the Cork Furniture Store in Cork city's Merchant Street. After some years of trading, the store expanded and began to sell ladies' clothes as well as furniture. In 1919, he purchased The London House, which was one of the biggest and best-known stores on St Patrick's Street. In September 1919, the store was renamed Roches Stores Ltd. The business was destroyed during the burning of Cork in 1920 but soon reopened in a temporary setting. The new premises were completed in January 1927. Over the ensuing decades, Roches Stores became a national chain of department stores in the Republic of Ireland. In 2006, Debenhams acquired the business. Up until the takeover, the Roche family retained full ownership of the stores.

STRANDED

On 18 April 1983, Captain Ruben Ocana, flying a Gulfstream II with four passengers made an emergency landing at Mallow Racecourse. Shannon Airport was the destination but on the day, fog descended upon the region.

While rerouting to Cork Airport, the captain ran low on fuel and identified the racecourse as a potential landing site. Locals witnessed the emergency landing in awe of the skill that the pilot had to deploy in order to land on a grassy site. The landing made local and national news. It also became very apparent that to get the plane back in the sky, a giant runway would need to be constructed.

Captain Ocana was warmly welcomed by the town of Mallow and given a room in the Central Hotel to await the completion of the runway. The pilot became a celebrity of sorts in the town and was even given the privilege of judging a beauty pageant! The Mexican pilot and his crew were stranded in Mallow for thirty-nine days.

RTÉ reporter Pat Butler visited Mallow to talk to Captain Ocana and to follow the progress of the building work adjacent to the racecourse. A temporary tarmacadam runway of over 900m in length was laid to enable the aircraft to leave, five weeks later in May. It was built by the Irish Sugar Company and had to be dug 7m deep for insurance purposes, costing in the region of €200,000. Two thousand people turned up to see the plane taking off again, bound for Mexico.

As the years progressed, Captain Ocana had hoped to revisit Mallow, but he sadly died in 2009, aged 81, without realising his dream. On 7 July 2010, his daughter Mariana respected her father's wishes with an emotional trip to the racecourse to meet witnesses and those who had helped the captain leave again on his plane.

SURVIVAL

In the days of piracy and buried treasure, the town of Kinsale hosted one sailor whose story has inspired books, films and tales of struggle for survival against rough environments.

Near the lower cove on the coastal pathway there is a plaque indicating the visit of Scotsman Alexander Selkirk to Kinsale. In 1703, he was a crew member of *Cinque Ports* as the ship remained at anchor in the harbour before setting out on a voyage into history. Captain Thomas Stradling was the ship's captain. A few weeks after departing from Kinsale, Captain Stradling accused Selkirk of provoking the crew to mutiny through his questioning the safety of the vessel. Angry that his authority had been challenged, the captain threatened to leave any potential mutineers on shore. Dissent quickly evaporated, but Selkirk continued to object, so the angry captain gave his problematic crew member a rifle, a knife and a Bible and dumped him on an isolated island in the Caribbean.

Four years later, Captain Woode Rogers of Bristol wandered into the lost island territory. Rogers was employed by the king to sail from the port to the Caribbean on board the *Duke* to clear the high seas of pirates. On 1 February 1709, running short of fresh water, Captain Rogers landed on Juan Fernandez, a small uninhabited island off the coast of Chile.

As the crew waded ashore, the gaunt figure of Alexander Selkirk tumbled out of the undergrowth giving praise to the Lord for his rescue. During his isolation he had built a shelter, killed wild goats, nurtured wild cabbage and turnips and read from the Bible.

Captain Rogers was so amazed by Selkirk that he hired him as mate of the ship on the return journey to Britain. Back in Bristol, the captain entertained his seafaring colleagues with stories of the escapades of Selkirk. Captain Rogers was a friend of London-based political author and journalist Daniel Defoe. In 1719, Defoe published a novel titled *Robinson Crusoe*, based on the Selkirk ordeal.

The Scottish sailor also penned an account of his years living on the island and resumed his seafaring career in the Royal Navy. While serving as a lieutenant on board *Weymouth*, Selkirk contacted yellow fever and died in Plymouth on 13 December 1721, aged only 45.

SWIM

Dotted around the coast of County Cork are many pretty bays and coves. A few are situated in the midst of beautiful scenery; some have broad expanses of golden sands. One such site of note is Myrtleville Beach near Crosshaven.

With the loss of the area's Coastguard service at the time of the First World War, Myrtleville lost much of its importance, but then came the advent of days of family summer holidays to which thousands of Cork people flocked.

One Cork businessman constructed no fewer than five houses, the first two of timber but the others much more extensive. All five were inhabited every summer. Another well-known Cork citizen erected a large timber house, which was made primarily of wartime buildings that the American Navy had at Aghada while they were stationed there during the First World War.

That was in the 1920s and early '30s, but for quite a few years there were not more than a dozen or two holiday houses at Myrtleville. Most of them bore musical names – Byways, Kantara, Gweedore, Myrtle Cottage, Fuschiaville, etc.

In those days, it was still a curiosity to see a motor car come down to Myrtleville around a rough, hilly road. Up to 1932, one travelled by train to Crosshaven and then trudged the long road to Graball Bay, Church Bay, Fennell's Bay, Myrtleville or even farther afield to Fountainstown.

A decade earlier, the wagonette had been the popular mode of conveyance for the Cork family going to the beach. The head of the household hired a wagonette for the day and packed his spouse, children (with buckets and spades), bedclothes, pots and picnic for a trip to the beach.

The building of the cliff road to Fountainstown was a crucial event in the history of Myrtleville. Up to 1930 or so it ran only to Poulgorm, with a footpath or cart track continuing on along the cliff over Shell Hole. To transform this track into a roadway was a bold enterprise – and for the private contractor who realised it, it was an expensive one. Sand, earth and gravel for the new road were taken up the cliff from the seashore at Shell Hole on trolleys by pulley, operated by an old motor car engine high in the cliffs.

Tasteful rockeries were constructed on the approach to the strand. Those were the activities of the Myrtleville and Bays Development Co., Ltd, a group formed under the Tourist Act of 1953. They also acquired the old boat house and equipped it as a shelter for those caught out in a sudden summer rain shower. This company, headed by Gus Healy, a Cork City Councillor, was the successor to the Poulgorm Improvements Committee, which, in the 1930s carried out such simple but essential tasks as providing pathways through the rocks and small shelters at Divore (near Shell Hole), Poulgorm, Myrtleville and Fennell's Bay. They pioneered to make Myrtleville one of the best-loved seaside locations in County Cork, which it still is.

SWORD

The doctor's sword in McCarthy's Pub in Castletownbere has been the subject of many newspaper articles and documentaries. Born in Castletownbere in 1913, Dr Aidan McCarthy went on to study medicine in the 1930s at Dublin's Clongowes Wood College. This was a private establishment and it was here that Aidan developed his love of rugby. Due to a shortage of work, Aidan emigrated to Wales and then moved to England.

At the advent of the Second World War, the widespread call to join the Allied forces in the war against Germany led Aidan to sign up. He joined the Royal

Air Force as a medic and soon was placed on the battlefront to tend to the most horrific of injuries.

Aidan was one of those soldiers on a ship being evacuated from Dunkirk to the English coast. His own vessel was torpedoed, which caused numerous fatalities. It was a miracle the terribly smashed up ship limped back to England. On board, Aidan, with other colleagues, was doing his best to help seriously injured soldiers in crude operating spaces.

Next up, Aidan was sent to Japan, a then British colony. RAF hurricanes were dispatched to fight off Japanese bombing raids. The Allied cause was not successful and thousands of soldiers were captured and imprisoned in prisoner-of-war camps on the adjacent island of Java. Physical and psychological torture, executions, as well as food rationing was commonplace.

Once again Aidan's skills as a doctor were called upon. He created diets to try to prevent the spread of malaria and dysentery. He also snuck in yeast cultures concealed in rice balls so they could be used to create protein drinks for the ill.

In 1944, with the dynamic nature of the war, Japan moved its prisoners of war to the mainland to work in its factories. In April 1944, the ship carrying Aidan and 980 other prisoners was hit by a torpedo from a US battleship. Forty prisoners were killed, and Aidan clung to the ship's wreckage until another Japanese destroyer arrived.

However, the Japanese rescue boat chose just to save the Japanese crew and Aidan was forced to jump off the deck and take his chances at sea. This time, he was rescued by a whaling vessel and taken to Nagasaki, where he was detained in another prisoner-of-war camp. There he was subject to horrific beatings.

When the Americans dropped an atomic bomb on Nagasaki, Aidan was luckily in an air-raid shelter. Emerging from that, he was taken again to another hard-labour camp.

Shortly afterwards, the Emperor of Japan surrendered to the Allied forces. As his own peace offering, Aidan locked the camp commander in a room for his own personal protection from other prisoners of war. The camp was eventually liberated and the commander handed Aidan his ceremonial sword in gratitude for the protection.

Aidan retired from the RAF and opened a general practitioner's space at home in Castletownbere. Today, the sword can be viewed in McCarthy's Pub.

TABLE

The Kerryman's Table is a large rock jutting from a natural ditch on the old Butter Road from Killarney to Cork and positioned about 5km east of Millstreet. The rock table was a gathering point for the carman, or cart man, of the nineteenth century. It was a meeting place for them and their horses as they carried their produce to the Cork Butter Market and returned with provisions for themselves and shops in Killarney, Castleisland and Kenmare as well as in Millstreet. The trade added considerably to the development of Millstreet and did much to safeguard the areas it served from the worst impacts of Ireland's Great Famine years.

There was much devotion to the packing and handling of the butter in the strong firkins that were eminently suited for long journeys. The firkin was conveyed in the farmer's cart to the nearest village or town and there handed over to the carman, who was in direct touch with the Cork Market. The carman generally took three or four horses on the road and either personally attended to the entire details of the work during the journey and subsequent delivery at the market or else came up to town and made sure everything was OK for the journey. The carmen usually travelled in convoy.

Halts were made for the refreshment of both men and horses at the various stage houses on the route or sites such as Kerryman's Table. The stage houses were, as a rule, licensed premises, and were mainly survivors of the old stage-coaching dwellings. Further lodging houses in the city as well as accommodation for the horses were required while waiting for the butter to be inspected and payment given – and then there was the journey back home.

TALL

There are many well-worn spots in Gougane Barra where people stop to photograph the lake, the mountains and the forestry. A state-supported project here was that of the Irish Free State Forestry Programme in the late 1930s.

Subsequently, the forest area became Ireland's first national park in 1966.

An interesting anecdote on the forestry in Gougane Barra appeared in the *Irish Independent* on 2 January 1968. It notes:

> When GAA field activities are resumed the task of umpires at Croke Park games will be considerably easier than in the past, when it was often difficult to determine if a ball, particularly in hurling had gone wide or was within the posts. They replaced the 25 feet high uprights with 35 feet high posts, which were erected when the Croke Park pitch was re-sited in 1959, consequent to the construction of the Hogan Stand.

The GAA General Secretary Seán Ó Siocháin first got the idea of the new posts when on holiday in Gougane Barra during the summer of 1968. There he saw spruce trees standing over 18m high and considered that their height would be ideal for goal posts.

TORCH

Youghal Lighthouse presents a striking scene to photograph. Its predecessor, though, was a basic and small tower, which was operated by a religious order of nuns of St Anne's Convent. It is speculated that they may have been members of the Second Order of St Francis. One of Ireland's earliest Franciscan friaries was established in Youghal.

Maurice Fitz-Gerald is said to have constructed the tower and handed it over to the care of the nuns with the clear-cut understanding that they would look after it. Reputedly, before the arrival of the nuns, the Youghal coastline was dangerous for ships to negotiate. Local malefactors would even lure ships onto the rocks, so their cargoes could be looted. Once the nuns were installed as guardians of the tower, captains could have confidence in the huge torches. Night after night, they kept the torches steadily lit so the light could beam out through the tower's two large circular-headed windows.

Local folklore also outlines that there may have been an underground passage from the convent to the sea. This would have helped make sure the torches were not blown out before they made it to the lighthouse. The nuns were in charge of the light tower and the convent existed until 1542. At that point, the building was unable to endure the exertion of the storms any longer. A new, sturdier lighthouse was built on the site.

TORNADO

Tales of mini tornadoes appear every now and again in the coastal history of County Cork. For example, on 5 December 1908, the lobster boat *Water Lily* was in the Long Island channel of Roaringwater Bay. It was heading westwards towards the island, the home of skipper John O'Driscoll, who was with his 18-year-old son Jack. Accounts of the events that followed have been passed down within the community. These recall a moderate breeze and no awareness of any apparent danger from a sudden squall.

John O'Driscoll saw a second boat, belonging another local fisherman, John O'Donovan, ahead of the *Water Lily*, so he and his son tightened their gig's mainsheet to catch it. Thus preoccupied, they failed to see a vortex rapidly approaching from behind. Jack remembered his father's shout to let go the mainsheet before it overwhelmed them. John O'Driscoll drowned, but his son was rescued by a boat put out from the island, where the waterspout and its moving mist of foam had been seen and watched with horror by some of the islanders.

TRAINING

In 1883, the British Army began hosting training manoeuvres at Kilworth, whose terrain was deemed good for the purpose. Soon after, the British War Department bought extensive plots of land there. In 1886, the initial rifle range was unveiled on the site. The training operation continued to expand and the British soon created a permanent camp at the site. It was heavily used for troops preparing for battle in the Second Boer War of 1899 to 1902.

During the First World War, the camp became an even larger training ground. During the Irish War of Independence, Irish Republican prisoners were held at an internment camp at the site. In October 1921, several prisoners escaped by digging a tunnel underneath the huts and then the surrounding barbed-wire fence. In early 1922, the British relinquished control of the camp to the Provisional Irish Government. However, the Irish Civil War led Anti-Treaty forces to mount assaults on the Pro-Treaty camp holders.

During the Second World War, Kilworth hosted a training hub again for Irish troops. In the years after 1960, the camp became well known for training troops heading for missions of UN peacekeeping.

In 1966, to commemorate the fiftieth anniversary of the Easter Rising, the camp was named after General Liam Lynch. Liam had a prominent role in north Cork in the Irish War of Independence but after the Anglo-Irish Treaty became Chief-of-Staff of Anti-Treaty forces. On 10 April 1923, in the Knockmealdown mountains, he was shot and killed by Free State soldiers.

In 1969, Lynch Camp became a refugee camp for many Catholics who had escaped rioting in Northern Ireland. Today, Lynch Camp is one of the Irish Defence Force's busiest training centres. It has been renovated to quarter 320 troops for exercise practices at any one time and now has state-of-the-art catering and fitness facilities. Around 4,500 members of the Defence Force will come to Kilworth for training annually. There is an infantry training school, cadet school, a Reserve Defence Force and a non-commissioned officer training wing, which are spread across the area's 6,000 acres.

TRANSMISSION

Mullaganish Mountain lies just outside Ballyvourney. It is well known for its historic television transmitters. In 1962, Telefís Éireann's initial five core television transmitters went on air across the country. The County Cork site was one of these. By September 1963, the 170m mast transmitter could boast a 625-line VHF service for Ireland's south-west counties of Cork, Kerry and Limerick.

In 2009 a new mast was constructed at Mullaghanish. With its height of 225m, it was erected to assist with the rollout of the transmission of digital terrestrial television. The height made it Ireland's tallest television transmitter. The previous 170m mast was removed.

On 24 October 2012, analogue television transmissions from the Mullaghanish site concluded. It was replaced by the national digital terrestrial television, Saorview, which broadcasts at an effective radiated power (ERP) of 200kW. It is now the most powerful transmitter in all of Ireland. Six national FM radio services are broadcast from the site. Local station Radio Kerry is also broadcast from a western-facing antenna.

The topography of the area is difficult, though, and twenty relays are used for the transmitter to be effective. The company 2RN, a subsidiary of RTÉ, now owns and operates the site.

TUNNEL

At a height of 366m above sea level, the impressive and historical Caha Pass tunnel marks one of the routeway entrances between Cork and Kerry. Created in the 1830s, the hand-hewn pass is named after a local landowner called Turner. On the Kerry side, the main tunnel is followed by three more mini-tunnels, a set of twin tunnels and a final short tunnel. These were constructed as relief works for local labourers and as a means to open up new tourist routes from the 1830s onwards into south Kerry. One could only imagine the exhilaration of passing through Turner's Tunnel on horse and carriage and later by motor bus.

One hundred years ago, Turner's Tunnel was the subject of many photographers and postcard makers. They also wished to capture the O'Connor family, who lived in the adjacent cottage on the Cork side. In particular, Mary O'Connor is shown in front of the tunnel and her cottage, and she and her husband Patrick operated a teashop.

Mary and Patrick were a young local couple. She was from Derryconnery, Glengarriff, and he was from Innisfoyle, Bonane, near Kenmare. They were 22 and 25 years of age respectively when they married in 1905. They acquired the small cottage from a relative and built a two-storey house beside it. By all accounts, the teashop was successful. Mary and Patrick had a captive tourism market.

By 1910–15 Mary and Patrick had earned enough to improve the house and cottage. Their improvements included adding an upper floor to the cottage, which they then linked at first-floor level across the gap to the main house. They bricked up the space below the link and plastered the two buildings as one. This space was used for storage and access to it was by way of a ladder from a trapdoor at the first level in what was the children's bedroom. The decision to leave a gap at ground level was probably taken on grounds of cost: inserting lintels into two drystone walls would not have been easy or cheap. Whatever the reason for the now enclosed and concealed space, it was to prove significant later.

The period from mid-1920 to early 1921 was a fraught time in west Cork. In the summer of 1920, RIC constables had been killed in Bantry and Glengarriff; the Tooreen Ambush and its aftermath in Bandon took place in October; and the Bloody Sunday Massacre in Dublin and the Kilmichael Ambush both took place in November. Martial law was declared in Cork, Kerry, Limerick and Tipperary in December and the centre of Cork city was burned down by the Black and Tans. Incidents were many, and curfews were in place.

Tunnel and Café at Caha Pass, *c.*1900. (Cork Public Museum)

In Glengarriff, the British were concerned that suspected IRA Volunteers could disappear between Glengarriff and Kenmare, particularly at night. They had no idea where the Volunteers might be hiding, and the remoteness and isolation of the countryside where the road crossed the Caha Mountains seemed to provide excellent cover.

The Tunnel Cottage was one of the very few houses on the road once Glengarriff was left behind, but it does not appear that the teashop was suspected as a hideout. It looked innocent enough. It was a successful business in a substantial building, run by a young family that included six young children.

Mary and Patrick were an affable pair and provided refreshments to all travellers, including military personnel passing by. However, unbeknownst to these customers, their hosts used the space between the two houses to hide active service Volunteers. One of Mary's daughters later recalled to her own children how her bed and the rug beneath it would be moved, and men would go down into the space below. Then her bed would be moved back, and she would go back to sleep.

In February 1921, Mary was in the late stages of pregnancy. On the night of 18 February, she began to haemorrhage. Curfew notwithstanding, Patrick knew that he had to get a doctor urgently and he rode to Glengarriff. Unfortunately, he ran into a patrol, which, instead of helping him get the doctor, arrested him for breaching the curfew. He was then detained overnight and questioned about his movements and, perhaps, about what he knew about the ability of the Volunteers to disappear.

The next morning there came into the station an English officer who happened to have stopped in at the Tunnel Cottage teashop a little time before. He had seen that Mary was heavily pregnant and was able to confirm Patrick's reason for breaking the curfew. He ordered Patrick's release and provided an escort for Patrick and the doctor to return to the Tunnel. Sadly, they were too late. By the time Patrick arrived home Mary had died from 'shock and haemorrhage', as the death certificate recorded.

UNDERGROUND

The Oven Caves are situated on the south line of road from Cork to Macroom and is bounded on the north by the River Lee and intersected by the River Bride. Legend has it that it was here St Finbarr entered a 'darkness', or caves, before arriving in Corcach Mór na Mumhan, or the Great Marsh of Munster (now the site of Cork city).

The name Ovens is supposed to be a shortened form of Athnowen, derived from Ath-na-huamhann, or the Ford of the Caves. Samuel Lewis, in his *Topography Dictionary of Ireland* in 1837, notes of the caves and landscape here:

> It comprises 4660 statute acres, as applotted under the tithe act, and valued at £7594 per annum: the soil in the northern or hilly part is rather poor and stony, but in the vales extremely rich, lying on a sub-stratum of limestone forming part of the great limestone district extending to Castlemore on the west, and to Blackrock on the east. The limestone is quarried to some extent for burning into lime for the supply of the hilly districts to the north and south for a distance of several miles.

Charles Smith, in his *History of Cork* in 1750, described some of the caverns as being 18ft in height. Some of those he viewed branched off into several ramifications and from the roofs of some of them extended stalactites of various forms. He noted that he travelled underground for a quarter of an English mile and quoted from Virgil's *Aeneid* as a warning to careless explorers who will venture underground without the twine or thread guide. The local people he spoke with detailed that the cavern could be traversed as far as Carrigrohane and Gillabbey in Cork city.

John C. Coleman, historian and caver, wrote an article in 1940 on the Ovens Caves for the *Journal of the Cork Historical and Archaeological Society*. In the article, he refers to the entrance to the cave lying on the south side of a limestone quarry near the Ovens Bridge, about 3 miles west of Ballincollig. It appeared quarrying operations on the west side removed a significant portion of rock and possibly destroyed some of the ramifications of the cavern as known to the older explorers. There were several openings on the west side of the quarry but these were blocked on Coleman's visit and the opening on the south side was the only practicable entrance to the caves.

From the entrance, which is about 1m wide and 0.6m high, one scrambled along a low, wide passage, which led into a chamber. From here two main routes branched out and to the right a passage led to a Mass rock. There is a tradition that Mass was celebrated here during penal law days. According to John, the Mass rock chamber, which to all intents was the terminal chamber of the south route, was the most interesting place in Ovens Cave. The almost flat wall that faced the visitor as one entered and the similar roof were in striking contrast to the curved water-worn walls of the other parts of the cave. Coleman received suggestions from locals that the chamber was artificially enlarged to permit it being used as a chapel.

On the roof of the Mass rock chamber, Coleman viewed a thick deposit of soot scratched with many a name and date. Local people told him that the soot was caused by candles used at the Mass. The floor of the chamber was scattered with limestone blocks and dark clay and some of the stones, tabular in form, were noted by locals as the remains of an altar.

Coleman also referred to Dr Richard Caulfield, who visited Ovens Caves in 1864: 'Dr Caulfield visited the Ovens Cave in 1864, and in he notes that he and a Dr Fox dug the cave floor in several places and found bones and vertebrae in sequence, some fixed in the stalagmite floor.' Dr Caulfield felt that some of the bones found in the cave were thought to be human. John Windele, however, in his publication *Historical and descriptive notices of the city of Cork and its vicinity: Gougaun-Barra, Glengariff and Killarney* (1839), wrote of a Mr Francis Jennings who dug in several parts of the cave for fossils and other remains but made no discovery.

UNDERWATER

Between the afternoon of 20 April 1916 and the afternoon of the following day, Roger Casement attempted to land 20,000 guns and ammunition at Banna Strand, County Kerry, from a vessel really called SS *Libau* but masquerading as a neutral Norwegian merchant ship called SS *Aud*. The ship, on being escorted into Cork Harbour by the British Navy, was scuttled by its German naval officer, Captain Karl Spindler. On 30 June 1916 Casement was found guilty of high treason and sentenced to death on 3 August in Pentonville Prison.

Casement was in the British Consular service for eighteen years and was appointed British Commissioner to investigate the methods of rubber collection and the treatment of the native Indian tribes in the region known as Putumayo, on the Upper Amazon, a region dominated by the Peruvian Amazon Company. He relinquished the Consul-Generalship at Rio de Janeiro in 1913.

Casement took an active part in the Home Rule controversy in Ireland on behalf of the nationalist cause. He became a member of the Gaelic League in 1904. He was a skilled and determined networker in the lead-up to the Easter Rising. As the Home Rule crisis escalated, Casement resigned from the Foreign Office and devoted his energies openly to Irish independence.

After the founding of the Irish Volunteers in 1913, Casement spoke at recruitment rallies across the country and accompanied Pádraig Pearse, Tomás MacDonagh and Eoin MacNeill in building up the movement. In late July 1914, by then in the USA, he heard about the successful landing at Howth of guns by Erskine Childers and Mary Spring-Rice. His significant role in the planning of this venture gave him access to the inner circle of Clan na Gael (an Irish Republican organisation in the USA), and in November 1914, with the support of the IRB (Irish Republican Brotherhood) executive, he arrived in Berlin to promote and explain the Irish struggle, both politically and intellectually. His efforts to recruit and train an Irish brigade from among the Irish-born British Army prisoners of war in Germany failed. In April 1916, returning to Ireland, Casement was captured at an old ringfort near Banna Strand and stood trial for high treason.

Casement's body was returned to Ireland in 1965 and despite his wishes to be buried in his ancestral home in Antrim, he was buried in Glasnevin, Dublin. As for the *Aud*, it now lies broken up in 36m of water in Cork Harbour. There are a number of boilers to be seen as well as thousands of bullets strewn on the sea floor. Two of its fully restored anchors are now located at Tralee's Brandon Conference Centre and some of the guns and bullets are on display at Spike Island Heritage Centre.

UNDERWORLD

The Bull Rock Lighthouse, built on the largest and most westerly of a group of islets 4.8km off Dursey Head, is 83m above high water. The rock itself is precipitous and is perforated in an east–west direction by an arched tunnel, some 18m high, through which the seas sweep. The other islets are named Cow, Calf and Heifer, and the first of the group to be lit by a lighthouse was the Calf in the year 1865.

Teach Donn is commonly connected with Bull Rock. In Irish mythology, Donn is a god of the dead and the rock's archway is said to be a portal for the souls of the dead to depart through westwards, over the sea with the setting sun.

Donn derives from the Celtic word '*Dhuosnos*', meaning 'dark lord'. He is said to live in Teach Duinn, translated as 'house of the dark one'. It is where the souls of the dead gather before journeying to a final destination in the otherworld, or before one is reincarnated.

Other folklore connected to writers who assembled the *Leabar Ghabála Éireann* or *The Book of Invasions* say that Donn was one of the mythical ancestors of the Gaels. They are said to have invaded Ireland. Donn is said to have insulted Eriú, one of the goddesses of Ireland. She is said to have drowned him in a shipwreck off the south-west coast. Donn's own godly qualities in turn then created Teach Donn.

UNFINISHED

Kanturk Castle emerges strikingly above the trees of a wood lying to the south of Kanturk town itself. It is known locally as McDonough's Folly. The building was never finished and therefore never garrisoned or attacked. This has allowed Kanturk Castle to endure as a great example of Irish architecture dating from the very beginning of the seventeenth century. In recent years, the Office of Public Works has carried out extensive repairs and restorations and today the castle and its grounds are open to visit.

UNITED

In the heart of Astna Square in Clonakilty lies a fine limestone statue designed by John F. Davis and erected in 1898 to commemorate the centenary of the 1798 Rebellion, in particular, the men who died at the Battle of the Big Cross, near Clonakilty. The square is named in honour of the leader of the insurgents, Tadhg O'Donovan Astna.

On Tuesday morning, 19 June 1798, the sun shone down upon a historic gathering in west Cork of 300-400 pikemen. There was a forlorn hope that, had they been victorious, larger numbers in south-west of Ireland might have rebelled against the hold of the British Empire.

They lay in ambush on a scrubby hillside near the village of Ballinascarty, in an old ruined ringfort. Beside them were the copse woods of Lisselane demesne, and beneath them the main road from Clonakilty to Bandon ran for 1.6km between green meadows to the village. Opposite was a low ridge up which a byroad wandered towards Timoleague Abbey – hence the place names of the Big Cross or Croppies' Cross Roads.

The ringfort was crowded with insurgents – O'Donovans and the O'Heas and Collins from the sea coast and the Hurleys and Crowleys from the mountains. All carried a pike – 3m of stout ash with a spear point for thrusting, an axe blade for slashing, and a back hook for dragging down the enemy. A few of them had blunderbusses or old cavalry pistols and many wore the old Irish high felt hat and great frieze coat – the latter being tough enough to turn the point of a bayonet.

They were waiting to attack the Westmeath Militia on their 19km march from Clonakilty to Bandon. As the sun rose higher, the distant throb of drums warned them that their time had come to attack. The hidden insurgents watched as Colonel Sir Hugh O'Reilly appeared, riding a thoroughbred hunter at the head of his regiment. Behind him marched the Grenadier Company and two 6-pounder cannons trundling along in the rear. There were over 200 militiamen.

As they passed with their backs to the ringfort, pikemen leaped up with a wild cry and surged down upon the redcoats. Amidst hoarse shouting of orders and many a round oath, the astonished column wheeled around to face the stabbing of the pikes by violent thrusts. However, the militarily skilled redcoats turned the tables quite quickly and soon the pikemen were forced to retreat.

Tadhg O'Donovan Astna led a body of pikemen in a daring dash at the cannons to seize them. They nearly succeeded but Tadhg was shot dead.

At that moment another corps of Irishmen appeared on the ridge with the situation being in flux. Suddenly, the singing of bagpipes heralded the advance of a Scottish company of the Caithness Legion of Fencible Highlanders, who had marched 14.5km of bleak mountain road on their route from Bandon to Clonakilty. Round a bend of the road they swung in a rolling cloud of dust – 100 in all.

Under the orders of Major Innes, the legion formed a line three deep and, rapidly presenting their muskets, they fired at the pikemen of Carbery, who stood leaderless at the ringfort. The bombardiers made their cannon thunder again. When the dense smoke rolled away, all the pikemen were gone – their pikes could not contend with artillery. Upwards of 100 of them lay dead.

1798 United Irishmen Monument,
Clonakilty, present day.
(Cork Public Museum)

USE

Glanworth Bridge crosses the River Funshion on the eastern environs of Glanworth village. It has been recorded by some as 'the oldest and narrowest working bridge in Europe'.

The bridge is a historic humpbacked road bridge measuring about 3.75m wide, built in 'random-rubble' limestone with piers constructed on rocky outcrops in the river's bed. It has thirteen semicircular arches, which generally increase in width and size towards the centre. Ireland's National Inventory of Architectural Heritage records the detail of the structure: 'It has rough limestone voussoirs and low pointed cutwaters on the upstream side only. The span of the arches vary from 4.2m to 5.5m, and the width of piers from 1.5m to 2.4m. There is also a random-rubble parapet wall with the remains of vertical stone coping.'

The bridge is traditionally dated to 1446 and was one of several multi-span bridges at one time in Ireland. Many of the latter have not survived, which makes Glanworth Bridge unique.

Nearby the bridge is the striking thirteenth-century Glanworth Castle. It was constructed by the de Cauntetons, or Condons but in the fourteenth century it was taken over by the Roche family until the middle of the seventeenth century. An adjacent abbey was established by the Roches for Dominican Friars by 1475.

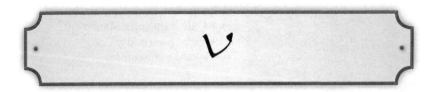

VANISH

Loughaderra Lake is one of the most scenic landmarks near Castlemartyr in east Cork. Folklore has it that where the lake is now situated was once covered by a compact, dark oak wood. It was part of the estate of an Elizabethan seneschal (local agent of the crown) of Imokilly, who resided in and governed from the castle nearby.

After an Earl of Desmond incursion, the seneschal felt that there was local collaboration with the invaders. He assembled a large number of residents in the immediate locality, conducted a quick trial, pronounced them all guilty and executed them all in the local wood.

From that day of execution the place was considered by the public to be cursed, and within a year blight swept through the wood. In addition, during a stormy winter night desolation fell on Loughaderra. With the advent of daylight no sign of the tree or wood remained – only a broad span of water extending over where the trees grew.

VILLAGE

In June 1992, there was much curiosity when the miniature model village at Island Road, Inchydoney, was first proposed as an important tourist attraction. Five model makers were employed under a FÁS scheme (a government funded community employment and placement scheme) and became busy at work in the old Farm Products building in Casement Street, with Finbarr Hegarty as supervisor. It was initially proposed that models of important buildings in Clonakilty, Skibbereen and Bandon were to be made and included among the Clonakilty models would be Emmet Square, the church and post office, Old Mill, brewery and Pearse Street. The very first building to be modelled was the courthouse, at one-twentieth of the real size. The miniature village was officially opened on Saturday 9 July 1994, by President Mary Robinson and continues to draw crowds.

Section of model village, Clonakilty, present day. (Kieran McCarthy)

✳ ✳ ✳

In 1899, Cork County Council came into being and encountered a housing crisis. During the first decade of the twentieth century, many farm labourers needed housing. At the same time, it was claimed that the system of building a single cottage on land acquired from a farmer with the largest acreage in any given townland was inadequate to meet demand. It was further thought that erecting cottages in groups and each on an acre of land would do much to solve the housing shortage. In 1906, Cork County Council agreed to build four such groups, named model villages, at Bishopstown, Clogheen, Dripsey and Tower.

Dr Barter of St Anne's Hydro (spa) was prepared to give an acre for each house built in Tower. The three others were restricted to a quarter of an acre.

The scheme for Dripsey began in 1910 and comprised sixteen cottages. Cork County Council acquired the land from Maurice Ring of Lismahane. The scheme was officially named Dripsey Model Village. In 1911, fourteen of the houses were allocated to farm labourers and two cottages to non-farm labourers.

VINDICATION

Mary Wollstonecraft was governess to the King children in Mitchelstown Castle. When she took on the post in 1786, she was aged 27. She had just completed a book (though not then published) called *Thoughts on the Education of Daughters*.

Mary's stay and work at Mitchelstown Castle was to last only a year, because Lady Kingsborough became resentful of her impact on her daughter, Margaret. Mary, after leaving Mitchelstown, continued to correspond with Margaret King, her favourite pupil.

In 1796 Mary married William Godwin. Their daughter, Mary, became the second wife of the poet Shelley and her life came to be closely interwoven with that of her mother's pupil, Margaret King. Margaret had married four years after her governess had been dismissed from Mitchelstown. At the age of 19 she married Stephen Moore, of Moore Park, County Cork, 2nd Earl of Mountcashel, who was 21 years of age.

Mary had her retaliation on the King family by putting a portrait of Lady Kingsborough into a later book called *A Vindication of the Rights of Woman*, as well as providing a commentary on her character: 'The wife, mother and human creature were all swallowed up by the factitious character which an improper education and the selfish vanity of beauty had produced.' Lady Kingsborough no doubt read the description of herself, for Mary's book became highly popular and was widely read.

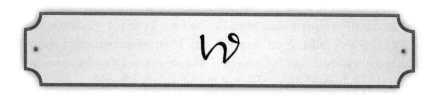

WALK

The defeat of the united forces of the Spanish and Irish at the Battle of Kinsale in 1601 led to one of the longest and most deadly walks in Irish history. The O'Sullivan Beara Gaelic clan were driven out of the Castletownbere region by the English.

Seeking sanctuary, Dónal Cam O'Sullivan, chieftain of the clan, began the long march to Leitrim on 31 December 1602. He led 1,000 men, women and children, who constituted a large-scale flight of people from the Castletownbere region.

In the middle of January 1603, the clan eventually arrived at their destination with only thirty-five people surviving. Many had been killed en route, were overcome by exhaustion, or came down with a lethal illness. Others disconnected from the long walk northwards and settled along the route.

In Leitrim, O'Sullivan requested to unite with other northern chiefs to battle English forces. However, Hugh O'Neil, the Earl of Tyrone sought peace and swore an oath of loyalty to the Crown. O'Sullivan and other Irish leaders sought exile, and made their escape to France and then on to Spain.

WARRIOR

A beautiful long path with beech trees on both sides now leads to Saint Fanahan's holy well, where pilgrims can reflect on the life of the warrior monk, Fanahan.

The ancient *Book of Lismore* recalls the legendary life and time of a warrior monk named Saint Fanahan, who was born at Rathkealy, Fermoy in the early seventh century AD. His father's name was Finlog, and the *Book* notes that he was chieftain of a small number of areas consisting of a few acres of land, and was one of several people who were banished from Ulster. The reason for this, however, is not recorded.

The *Book* further outlines that when Fanahan was 7 years of age, his family sent him to a monastery in Bangor, County Down. There he was educated as a monk, and his tutor was its abbot, St Comgell. Fanahan pursued his education, and in the years that followed became abbot of the monastery himself.

As a result of his fiery temper, he clashed regularly with his fellow monks and was soon driven away from the monastery. Fanahan and some other monks moved to the province of Munster where Cathail Mac Aedh was king. The king, delighted with his new religious adviser, gave Fanahan free choice of where he wanted to locate a new monastery.

According to the *Book of Lismore*, Fanahan swapped his 'good soul' with the 'bad soul' of the King of Desise, which led to Fanahan searching to cleanse his new soul. This quest to repent for his sins led Fanahan to hire seven smiths to produce seven sicles, which Fanahan used to punish himself, thus earning back his place in heaven. The smiths in question refused to be paid, but requested the new monastery be called Brí Gobhann, i.e Smith's Hill.

The *Book of Lismore* notes that during Fanahan's self-punishment campaign, an angel is reputed to have appeared to him asking him to be involved in a quarrel between the King of Meath and his enemies.

Fanahan, alongside the king and his armies, subdued their opponents with ease. There is even a folklore reference that sparks of fire came out of Fanahan's mouth and were directed towards the enemy, and that his staff had magical powers to move objects.

Fanahan also made time to undertake a pilgrimage to Rome. It is reputed it was here that he made his confession and swore to leave behind his violent ways. Perhaps he knew he was approaching his own death, which happened in 664 AD.

Canonised in later centuries, Fanahan's feast day is on 25 November. His magic staff was secured in the Brigown round tower, where it was highly valued until a storm heavily damaged the tower in 1720.

WAVE

Cleena's Strand is located in between Ross Bay and Galley Head. Just out from the beach is a rock named Carrig Cleena, around which the waters possess a dark hue. Passed down folklore describes that Cleena, or Clíona, was queen of the Munster fairies and banshee of the Desmond kings in the Middle Ages.

One legend relates that Clíona was the daughter of Mannanán Mac Lir. He was an Irish sea god. The family is said to have lived in Tír Tairngire, an otherworldly paradise much like Tir na nÓg' (Land of Youth). In such lands, there was no sadness, no growing old, no dying and it was a place where everlasting youth reigned.

Another legend has it that Clíona lived near Carraig Chlíona, a noticeably huge rock in an isolated section of the parish of Kilshannig, near Mallow. She was deemed the most attractive woman in Ireland and possessed great seduction powers. One man who became knowledgeable about her powers decided to kill her. However, she transformed into a wren and disappeared. She is said to have appeared as three brightly coloured birds who sang so beautifully that they healed all ailments. Their powers were said to come from their diet of eating apples from an otherworldly tree.

St Fanahan's Well, Mitchelstown, present day. (Kieran McCarthy)

Another tale describes that Clíona eloped from Tír Tairngire with an attractive young warrior named Ciabhán of the Curling Locks. They disembarked at Trá Théite, the strand at Glandore. Ciabhán left her in his boat. A mighty wave came in and she drowned. This wave was later renamed Tonn Chlíona (Cliona's Wave). The wave is still deemed a loud and immediate harbinger of death for someone.

WHITE

The strange tale of the haunting white lady of Charles Fort has echoed through the ages in the Kinsale region. Colonel Warrender, the fort governor and a strict disciplinarian, had a daughter named Wilful. The girl was adored – as much as her father was feared – by everyone. She became engaged to a young officer, Sir Trevor Ashurst, and married him. After the reception the happy couple, glad to be alone, went for a stroll along the battlements. Observing some flowers growing on the rocks below, the bride casually said they would make an attractive posy. The husband said nothing but secretly committed to get them for her.

When Trevor returned later with a rope, the sentry offered to make the descent instead, provided Sir Trevor would change places while he was away. This was agreed to, but the task took a lot longer than expected, and the officer fell asleep. Meanwhile, Colonel Warrender had started off on his evening round of inspection. Having received no answer to his challenge from the huddled-up figure in the guard turret, he drew his pistol and shot him. He did not realise that in the gathering darkness it was his son-in-law he had killed.

When the dead man's body was brought back to the Governor's House, the distraught bride rushed out and threw herself over the battlements. Her father, in utter despair at the double tragedy, committed suicide in the early hours of the following morning. Wilful, the young bride, reputedly wanders the fort as a ghost known as the white lady.

WIND

At 3 p.m. in the afternoon of 6 January 1839 a small green cloud, as the old people described it, appeared over Cork Harbour. A little snow ensued but the place descended into darkness and then began what is described as the 'night of the big wind'. Cork was first in the path of the wind as it is situated in the south-west. The recorded damage was devasting and the story of the wind lingered on in living memory for decades.

In particular, much damage was done to houses and crops in west Cork. The *Cork Constitution* reported that: 'In the neighborhoods of Bandon, Skibbereen, Clonakilty, Bantry, &c., the storm raged with great violence, and houses are unroofed, and plantations ruined, and hay and corn blown about in every direction.'

There was a ship near Rerrin Pier in Bere Island pier called the *Brigg Henry*, which was reported as having been lifted clear out of the water, and a schooner called *Eliza* was put right up on a beach. All the boats in Cork Harbour sank, all the lights went out and no one could stir out. It is said that even the livestock in the fields were picked up like feathers and hurled along for miles.

In Burren, East Carbery, sand dunes were created when huge amounts of sand were blown up from the strand. The sand was blown up out of the strand in Kilbrittain's Harbour View and it buried houses at the north side of the road near Boat Cove. Estates were also denuded of timber – on Fota Island, Cork, over 1,000 trees were knocked over by the wind.

WINDOW

About 3km west of Rosscarbery, the Glandore road crosses through the valley of the River Roury. A central element of the landscape here is a seventeenth-century fortified mansion called Coppingers' Court, or Ballyvireen House, which stands as a ruinous monument to the man who was perhaps County Cork's most powerful magnate, Sir Walter Coppinger. Walter was a magistrate, lawyer, money lender and land speculator.

After the Battle of Kinsale in 1601, west Cork comprised large sections of land whose Irish owners had either absconded or were otherwise absent. Sir Walter came into the possession of their estates and within a few short years he owned a very large proportion of west Cork. His major plan, however, was focused on the Roury Valley, where he intended to develop a new town with an inland harbour. The plans did not reach fruition beyond the construction of his fine mansion house.

Part of the myth surrounding it is that it had a 'a chimney for every month, a door for every week, and a window for every day of the year'. Walter's land empire soon collapsed with the Irish Roman Catholic rising of 1641.

WIRELESS

While the accomplishments in Ireland of the Italian inventor Guglielmo Marconi (1874–1937) are linked more commonly with his first transatlantic telegrams from Clifden, County Galway, in October 1907, it is often discounted that at an earlier date he successfully led field trials at Crookhaven in west Cork, where his 'wireless station' was in operation from June 1901.

In Crookhaven, the station was located at Brow Head in an old Napoleonic watch tower. Marconi, who had set up other stations around the southern English and Irish coasts, arrived himself. While there, he established that Morse signals were clearly received from Cornwall, some 362km away. He discovered that the station's range was up to the planned 483km using a spark gap transmitter and detectors. Marconi was confident of 'bridging the Atlantic'.

The principal activity at Crookhaven was creating communications with seagoing vessels and most ships coming from the west and bound for European ports got in contact with Crookhaven, so it sprung into prominence as a wireless station. One of these, a steam ship, broke down some 128km west of the Fastnet Rock and sent out a distress call to Marconi at Crookhaven. When Marconi got details of the trouble, he phoned the shipyard engineers in Scotland, who relayed instructions through Marconi to the ship's engineers. The problem was solved.

The Crookhaven station started to fade out around 1914 but it had a very intriguing history and must have an important place in the history of wireless telegraphy. The site is now a ghostly ruin.

WITCHCRAFT

Witch trials have been rare in Ireland, but Cork courthouse hosted one on 11 September 1661. Accused of witchcraft, Youghal native Florence Newton stood trial. Sir William Ashton presided. The tale is outlined in a 1681 pamphlet entitled *Full and Plain evidence Concerning Witches and Apparitions in two Parts*. It was written by John Glanvil.

Mary Langdon was a key witness for the prosecution. The story begins during Christmas 1660 at the house of John Pyne, for whom Mary worked as a servant. Florence Newton was a guest and asked for a piece of beef, which was being cooked. Mary refused the request. A week later, the angst between the two was attempted to be resolved. Florence kissed Mary violently and noted, 'I pray thee, let thee and I be friends'.

Some weeks later, Mary began having fits and trances and began to vomit up things such as horse nails, needles, straw and wool. Apparitions also began. She also claimed that small stones would hit her and fall to the ground and disappear. Mary's fits only halted when Florence was imprisoned.

Another witness, Nicholas Stout, was called to give evidence at the court. Here the query of whether Florence could say the Lord's Prayer was raised. Florence was unable to recite the full prayer and was unable to say 'and forgive us our trespasses'. When the court enquired on why, she said that she was aged and had trouble remembering.

John Pyne, the householder, in his evidence noted that his servant Mary fell into violent fits, in particular if reading her Bible. The Bible would be oddly struck out of her hand and flung into the centre of the room.

Other witnesses were called, and the evidence became more extreme. The upshot of the trial remains unknown. However, there was much evidence to convict and punish Florence by either burning or hanging. No information to confirm her execution has ever come to light.

WREN

One of Munster's largest events for Wren Day, or Lá an *Dreoilín*, takes place in Carrigaline on St Stephen's Day. Annually, up to eighty-five people dress up. The Carrigaline Wren Boys Street Carnival has been hosted on Main Street, Carrigaline, for over twenty-five years.

The ancient tradition was revived by local man Barry Cogan, his family and friends. Wren Day is said to stem from Celtic mythology. The wren, known for its winter song, signified the close of the year, or the year past. Its association is so connected with Druidic ritual that the word for 'wren' in Irish is 'Dreolín', which could derive from the words '*Draoi*' and '*Éan*', meaning 'druid bird'.

Tradition has it that Wren Boys chased and stoned the winged winter creature. They then tied him to the top of a pole that the leader carried, and paraded this through the village with traditional *céilí* music. They would also go from door to door across the neighbourhood, asking for a penny for the wren's funeral. If homeowners were not forthcoming, they would run the risk of the Wren Boys burying the bird outside their house – a mark of bad luck. Payment would earn you a wren feather, which was good luck for the year to come.

Folklore also has it that it was a wren that alerted the Jews to where St Stephen was hiding, leading to his capture and death by stoning. It is also legend that when Oliver Cromwell's soldiers were asleep and the Irish were about to attack, a flock of wrens were disturbed and rose into the air to wake Cromwell's forces with the beating of their wings. Legend also suggests the same happened when Viking invaders arrived centuries before.

Nowadays, no wren is harmed in the process and a fake one is paraded. The Wren Boys then continue the chase through pubs and the hotel, where they will sing, play and dance as they go. The collection is generally in aid of Marymount Hospice and the Motor Neurone Disease Association. The South Union Hunt also holds its annual Carrigaline Meet on St Stephen's Day and leaves the Strand Road car park on horseback.

XENOMANIA

In the early nineteenth century coastal defences were built on Ireland's south coast to repel any potential Napoleonic invasion on Britain. On Garinish Island, off Glengarriff, a Martello tower and a fort or barrack building was constructed.

However, for several years after the military had left their base at Garinish, the island remained untenanted. In 1910 it was bought by a wealthy Belfast man and Liberal MP for Inverness, Annan Bryce. He regularly took his holidays in Glengarriff with his wife, Violet L'Estrange.

In essence, the 37-acre island comprised rock, heather and gorse, with some boggy parts. However, Annan Bryce transformed the landscape and built a house with surrounding ornate gardens across the island. He employed noted landscape architect Harold Peto. One hundred men were employed in blasting rock, digging out bog and building the Italian-themed garden.

The Bryces stayed for a long period in a cottage on the island overseeing the work and waiting for their mansion to be constructed. However, the mansion was not to be, as the First World War severely limited Bryce's finances. Expenditure on the gardens was slashed and the mansion concept was completely abandoned.

When Annan Bryce died in 1924, his widow Violet continued to reside at the cottage and oversaw the development of the gardens. The sheltered location and the temperate climate created a perfect setting for the magnolias, rhododendrons and camellias for which Garinish Island became famous.

Violet survived until 1939, but seven years before her death she gave the care of the island over to her son. Eventually, however, Roland Bryce, a brother of Annan, inherited the island and its gardens. He was Ambassador to the USA and on his death in 1954 he bequeathed the island to the Irish nation. The Office of Public Works then took responsibility for Garinish.

The island was known as Illauncullin, translated as 'the Island of Holly', which became shortened to Ilnacullin. This was the name always utilised by the Bryces. Through the years, the island name has been corrupted to Garinish Island.

Central garden and pond on Garinish Island, present day. (Kieran McCarthy)

* * *

Located near Castletownroche is Anne's Grove, which was the home of the Annesley family from the seventeenth century until 2015. At that point, it was gifted to the Irish Government and was taken into the care of the Office of Public Works (OPW). The OPW pursued large conservation works to the house, outbuildings and gardens so that they could be opened to the public.

The showcase by the OPW is the oldest part, which is the walled garden and which was initially laid out in the eighteenth century, while the woodlands garden section holds some of the earliest rhododendrons introduced to and grown in Ireland.

Most notably, the story of Richard Arthur Grove Annesley can be explored. He inherited Anne's Grove in 1892 and developed the landscape in a new style of gardening in the early twentieth century. He supported the plant-hunting expeditions led by Frank Kingdon-Ward to Tibet, Yunan Province, Burma and Bhutan. In return, Richard assembled an exotic collection of plants. Some of the impressive flowering shrubs dating from this period include *Cornus kousa*, embothrium, eucryphia and hoheria.

X MARKS THE SPOT

Ireland's tallest high cross is located atop Castlefreke and is known as Lady Carbery's Cross. Erected by Mary Freke in 1901 in memory of her husband, it has sweeping views over Long Strand to the distant Galley Head and as far west as the Fastnet Rock. The cross comprises 14 tons of white limestone and rises 30ft into the sky. There are seven panels, each of which has sculpted designs from the Bible. The inscription on the east face reads: 'To the greater glory of God, and in loving memory of Algernon William George, 9th Baron Carbery, who was born 9th September 1868 and who died 12th June 1898. This Cross has been erected by Mary, his wife, 1901. The souls of the righteous are in the hand of God, they are in peace.'

YANKS

In early September 1917, a coast-to-coast call for military men was made across the United States of America. The calls aimed for a quarter of a million men to enlist in the American forces on battle fronts in western Europe. Subsequently, between 1917 and 1919, thousands of US naval personnel ended up being stationed in Cork Harbour and Bantry Bay, engaging in the war against German U-boats and seeking to ensure convoy security.

In September 1917 in Queenstown (now Cobh), according to the diary of American Naval Commander Joseph Knefler Taussig, there were eight American destroyers – *Wadsworth, Porter, Shaw, Ericsson, Jacob Jones, Paulding, Burrows* and *Sterett* – all helping to convoy merchant ships in the Irish sea. Their wide web of facilities in the county by war's end comprised sites in Cobh, Passage West, Haulbowline (now the Irish Naval Service Headquarters), Ringaskiddy, Aghada, Bere Island, Berehaven and Whiddy Island. Aside from their storage and barrack sites, the Americans also set up training areas, recreational centres and a hospital.

The hundreds of sailors involved in these ships were quite the celebrity in the harbour and in Cork city. In July 1917, the officers of the Cork County Cricket Club wrote to the US Embassy in London offering their pavilion and grounds at the Mardyke to the Americans should they need them. The offer led the commanders of two of the Cobh-based vessels – USS *Melville* and USS *Trippe* – to think about staging a baseball match between their respective crews. It was decided to use it to raise funds to support the local Queenstown War Workers Fund. It was played on a midweek July afternoon before a crowd of 3,000 people. There were many American sailors among them, but the majority were local onlookers.

In addition, some newspaper reports (*Cork Examiner* & *Evening Echo*) noted that hundreds of young women each night were drawn to Queenstown to mix with those sailors on shore leave. That was enough to raise the tempers of some sidelined local men. In the city on Monday, 3 September 1917, a party comprised of young boys hissed and jeered at American sailors whom they chanced to meet.

It started in King Street (now MacCurtain Street). American sailors accompanied by young girls attracted the attention of several young men, who immediately vented their resentment by jeering. They followed them until quite a large crowd gathered and the girls and sailors parted. They passed another group of Americans, and the crowd directed their efforts against these. The crowd followed and jeered at them to the Lower Glanmire Road Railway Bridge. Here the police intervened and moved the crowd back towards King Street. Near the Coliseum, an American sailor, standing in the portico of the theatre, was the centre of attention. It transpired he was attacked by a group of youngsters.

Following the city incident, the American sailors were forbidden to come into Cork city. With restricted shore leave in Queenstown, there was a number of disturbances there involving American sailors and local civilians. The civilians displayed ill-feeling towards women from Cork city who had been travelling to Queenstown each night to meet the sailors.

American sailors at Queenstown (now Cobh) in 1917. (Cork City Library)

Z

ZEAL

The conclusion of the Napoleonic War between England and France in 1815 caused a huge economic downturn in Ireland and Britain. The economic depression that followed hit regions in different ways. West Cork was hard hit by a steep decline in the profitable trade of providing ships with butter and other provisions in Cork Harbour. Large numbers of the population became financially broke, with many unable to afford their rent. This led to many landlords sending in the local police to reclaim rents.

Many organised movements were created across Ireland, who battled any injustice. In 1822, secret societies such as the Whiteboys operated at night, pursuing raids against their persecutors and then returning home before dawn. They ran in numbers of twenty or thirty. They also created encampments across hills and camped there for long intervals.

In January 1822 the Keimaneigh Pass near Bantry was used as one of the west Cork locations for chance attacks targeting local landlords in the name of denouncing rent oppression. The method of attack was the throwing of rocks and hence the name Rockites was given to these large groups of men.

One account of the time speculates that there were 2,000 men at Keimaneigh and 5,000 in the camps, which lay between Macroom and Millstreet. Those numbers are probably inflated, but the bands were noticeably large.

The first occurrence in Keimaneigh happened during the night of Friday, 11 January. A gathering of about 500 Rockites stormed a number of the homes of gentry in the Bantry area, looking for weapons. They attained a number of muskets, but no ammunition.

The response by the gentry was swift. The following day, Saturday, 12 January, Lord Bantry and his brother Captain White amassed a group of about fifty Yeomanry and set out on horseback to find the Rockites. They were uniformed and armed with pistols and sabres.

Near Ballingeary, the Yeomanry came upon the Rockites but they scrambled into the hills and headed back on foot for the pass. Realising the threat to their

Pass of Keimaneigh, *c.*1930. (Cork Public Museum)

situation, the Yeomanry withdrew back through the pass, just in time to avoid the hail of stones flung down from the heights. They then rode back to Bantry.

There they considered what had happened, regrouped and set out once more at 5 a.m. on Monday, 21 January. Once more the Yeomanry encountered the Rockites. The Rockites totalled about 400 and were mostly armed with pitchforks or spades. They had about fourteen muskets, some very ancient, and little or no ammunition.

The resultant battle lasted all day. The mounted Yeomanry rode down towards Inchigeela and seized several captives, before turning back to rejoin the soldiers. The Rockites dodged the musket balls where they could. Once the soldiers had fired off all their ammunition, some irregular hand-to-hand fighting occurred. However, the Rockites ran to secure their position above the Pass, and readied themselves to bombard rocks down on the warring party.

Feeling they had lost the upper hand, the Yeomanry clambered through the pass before it was cut off by the danger of falling stones. A large foot party were forced to return to Bantry by the old Bantry road. This added about 30km to their day's marching.

By early February 1822, the Rockites abandoned their encampment in Keimaneigh and returned to their homes and farms. According to local lore, there were several factors such as fear of a larger reprisal group, shortage of food for being on the run and a cold winter of rain.

Local lore submits that the real number of Rockites killed was anything up to twelve people. Reprisals did take place. Lord Wellesley, the Lord Lieutenant in Cork city, set up a special commission to try the large number of prisoners taken at several affrays in Keimaneigh, Carriganimma, Deshure and Newmarket. Altogether thirty-six men were sentenced to be hanged.

Visit our website and discover thousands of other History Press books.

www.thehistorypress.co.uk